# Essential Hungary

by

MICHAEL IVORY

PASSPORT BOOKS
a division of *NTC Publishing Group*
Lincolnwood, Illinois USA

Published by Passport Books, a division of NTC Publishing Group, 4255 West Touhy Avenue, Lincolnwood (Chicago), Illinois 60646–1975 U.S.A.



Published by Passport Books in conjunction with The Automobile Association of Great Britain.

Written by Michael Ivory
"Peace and Quiet" section by Paul Sterry

Library of Congress Catalog
Card Number 93–85611
ISBN 0–8442–8914–0

10 9 8 7 6 5 4 3 2 1

PRINTED IN TRENTO, ITALY

*Front cover picture: Traditional costume*

The weather chart displayed on **page 102** of this book is calibrated in °C and millimetres. For conversion to °F and inches simply use the following formula:

25·4mm = 1 inch          °F = 1·8 x °C + 32

# Contents



This book employs a simple rating system to help choose which places to visit:

 'top ten'

 do not miss
◆◆ see if you can
◆ worth seeing if you have time

# Introduction and Background

## INTRODUCTION

Hungary is one of Europe's most rewarding destinations, the annual total of tourists far outnumbering the local population. Most visitors head for incomparable Budapest, the 'pearl of the Danube', or for romantic Lake Balaton in its frame of vineyards. Budapest is one of Europe's great capital cities, in an unrivalled setting of green hills and broad river, while Balaton, the 'Hungarian ocean', largest of the lakes of Central Europe, more than compensates for the country's lack of a coastline.

But Hungary is much more than a great city and a beautiful lake. The nation's unique and often troubled history gives it an identity unique in Europe. The Magyars' distant origin and unfamiliar language distinguish them from other Europeans. Their ancient, semi-nomadic skills and fine horsemanship are vigorously celebrated in the national parks of Hortobágy and Kiskunság, whose steppe-like landscapes are preserved in their primeval state. The Hungarian cuisine is also distinct, not to say distinguished, its fiery sauces and fine wines justification enough in themselves for your journey.

Hungary has spectacular and contrasting landscapes; the Danube Bend north of Budapest is one of the most splendid stretches in all the long course of the great river, while a first view of the vast expanse of Balaton can be breathtaking. But the most stimulating contrasts are perhaps those to be found in the differences between the capital and the cities and towns of the provinces, each with its own

*The view from Pest to beautiful Buda*

character, like sun-warmed Pécs, Art Nouveau Kecskemét, or the village-city capital of the Great Plain, Debrecen. The countryside is more varied still. The mansions and parks of a dispossessed nobility recall the days when one Hungarian in ten considered himself a nobleman. The open prospects and wide fields of state farms contrast with detailed vignettes of peasant life.

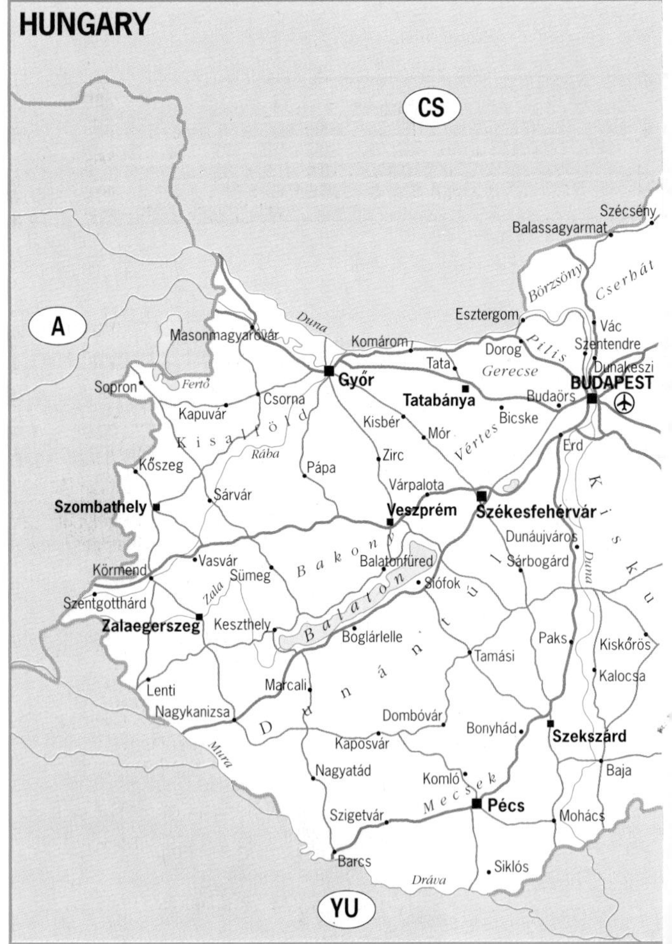

Except for the shortest of stays, you should not make the mistake of confining yourself to Budapest. The atmosphere of provincial places can only be fully savoured by those who stay in them, whether in a luxury hotel in an ancient city centre spared from destruction by the Turks, or on a campsite on some forgotten backwater of a remote river. Hungarian hospitality will make you welcome everywhere.

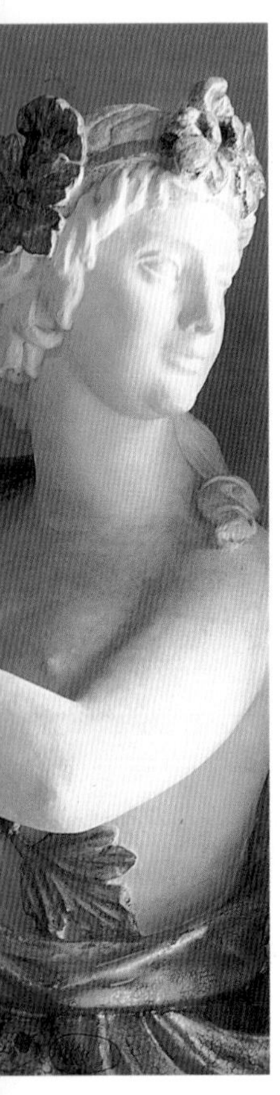

*A graceful figure in the Esterházy Palace, Fertöd*

## BACKGROUND

Landlocked Hungary is a small country, 35,900 square miles (93,000sq km) in area, with a population of well over 10 million, more than 2 million of whom live in Budapest, one of Europe's great metropolitan cities. The reason for the disproportionate size of the capital is to be found in the country's past; until the end of World War I the nation was three times its present size, stretching from the high peaks of the Carpathians to the blue waters of the Adriatic. Today, much reduced in area, Hungary sits squarely in the centre of the Carpathian Basin, with no high mountains and no outlet to the sea.

The Hungarian scene is a fascinating mixture of foreign influences and unique 'Hungarianness', reflecting an often uneasy balance between the country's vulnerable position in Europe and its constant strivings to achieve and express its own identity in the face of foreign influence and outright domination.

### Hungary Before the Magyars

Long before the arrival of the Magyars in AD876, the Romans had advanced through 'Pannonia' to the Danube, making the great river the frontier of their Empire. Some of the most impressive remains in Central Europe testify to the four centuries of the Roman presence here, notably the baths and amphitheatres of Aquincum just outside Budapest, the mosaics and altars of Szombathhely (Savaria to the Romans), and the mysterious underground mausoleums of Pécs (Sopianae).

### The Magyar Conquest

AD896 is the significant date in Magyar history. In that year their ancestors crossed the passes over the Carpathians and 'took possession' of the lowlands beyond, driving away or enslaving their mostly Avar or Slavic inhabitants. The leader of this conquest was the mighty Arpad; his demeanour and that of his companions in the fierce group of horsemen in Budapest's Heroes' Square is intended to remind you of the fear which the pagan Magyars inspired in the more settled folk of Christian Europe.

After a severe thrashing by the German armies of Otto the Great outside Augsburg in 955, a more stable existence took shape under the guidance of Prince Géza (reigned 972–97) and his son István (Stephen). Realising that the future lay in joining the civilised world, these wise statesmen saw to it that their country was Christianised. Stephen himself married a Bavarian princess, Gisela (Gizella), and his search for respectability was well rewarded in AD1000 when he was crowned king of Hungary by the pope and later canonised.

Medieval Hungary extended far beyond its present boundaries to include Transylvania (now in Romania), fertile lands along the Danube and Drava rivers (now in Croatia and Serbia), as well as an Adriatic coastline. To the north was the Felvidék, or Upper Hungary – mountainous country rich in mineral wealth (now Slovakia).

As in feudal England, tensions existed between monarch, barons, and the lesser nobility until limits were set by a compact known as the Golden Bull, signed in 1222, only a few years after England's Magna Carta.

Compared with most of Europe, little is left of Hungary's early Christian heritage; in the two terrible years of 1241–2, Mongol hordes stormed in from the east. Their trail of pillage and destruction spared neither people nor buildings. An intact early medieval church is an unusual sight in Hungary, making those that survived (like the lonely Cistercian abbey of Bélapátfalva at the foot of the Bukk uplands) doubly appealing.

**Hungary in Greatness**

But progress was resumed. By the mid-14th century, under Louis the Great, the frontiers of the realm had been pushed outwards and the Hungarian currency was the strongest in Europe. This period of greatness culminated in the reign of King Matthias. Under his long rule (1458–90) Hungary flourished economically and culturally. Matthias had followed the example of his famous father, János Hunyadi, in resisting the growing threat from the expansionist Turkish Empire to the southeast. After his death, things fell apart; his successors

*Matthias Corvinas: strong and just*

proved incapable of uniting the country, paying more attention to crushing the massive peasant revolt of 1514 than to the Turkish menace.

**Turkish Hungary**

In 1526 the Turks smashed King Louis II's army just outside Mohács in the south. Then followed the humiliating occupation of most of the country by the soldiers and pashas of the sultan. In spite of Turkish tolerance of the Christian religion, their century and a half of rule was a disaster for Hungary; though some towns continued to flourish as the Turks equipped themselves with the appurtenances of oriental civilisation like baths and mosques, much of the countryside was abandoned and fell into decay. Constant raiding prevented any sort of settled life in the broad border zone; consisting of a mere third of the country, this latter area stretched in a thin and vulnerable band from the foothills of the Alps in the west to Slovakia in the north. It was ruled by the Habsburgs, who, as well as reigning over Austria, had managed to install themselves firmly as Kings of Hungary, being crowned for that purpose in Pozsony (now Bratislava, Slovakia), the western city which perforce served as the Hungarian capital. It was they who finally drove the Turks out of Hungary altogether, to the accompaniment of much destruction. Buda was taken in 1686, and most of the rest of the country cleared by the end of the century.

**Habsburg Hungary**

Like other Hungarian 'liberations', the removal of the Turks proved to have been undertaken more in the interests of the liberators than the liberated. The Habsburgs were anxious to extend their domains and create a prosperous and obedient empire, while the Magyars hoped to recover their traditional pre-eminence. In pursuit of their aims, the Habsburgs brought in many settlers to repopulate the deserted countryside and help rebuild the devastated towns. Most of these new subjects of the Hungarian crown were German speakers, originating from all over Germany but known collectively as 'Swabians'. Their loyalty to the new rulers of the country could be relied upon, unlike that of the fractious Magyars, who rose in rebellion more than once. But local forces, however inspired, were no match for the imperial armies, who trudged stolidly round the country, smashing resistance and systematically demolishing the castles which might nurture future rebellions. Hungary's role under the Habsburgs was largely a matter of supplying agricultural produce to the rest of the Empire and of paying tribute to western ways. For well over a century after the liberation of Budapest, the crowning of a Habsburg as king of Hungary continued to take place in Pozsony/Bratislava, conveniently situated as it was a mere 40 miles (65km) or so down the Danube from Vienna.

This was the triumphant age of the baroque; fine churches and cathedrals, many of them designed and decorated by Austrians or Italians, were built, symbolising the gospel of the Roman Catholic Counter-Reformation now supplanting the Protestantism which had previously struck deep roots in this protest-minded country.

In the mid-19th century revolution broke out again, led by the demagogic journalist Lájos

Kossuth and inspired by the fiery young poet Sándor Petöfi. Successful at first, this renewed national uprising of the Magyars was eventually and brutally put down with the help of the Russian tsar. One reason for its failure was the unwillingness of some of the other minority groups in the country to join in what was perceived to be a Magyar-Habsburg struggle – an ill omen for future unity.

**The Compromise**

Less than two decades after the bitter defeat of 1848–9, by cleverly exploiting temporary Habsburg weakness, the Magyars seemed to have almost achieved their ambition for an independent existence. By the terms of the Compromise concluded with the government in Vienna in 1867, Hungary gained control over virtually all its affairs save defence and foreign relations. National confidence burgeoned: the country began to modernise itself in earnest and artistic activity of all kinds enjoyed a heyday. A wave of construction and reconstruction took place. Hitherto separate, the three cities of Buda, Óbuda (Old Buda) and Pest were fused into one in 1872; the newly created Budapest grew at a dizzy rate, becoming the undisputed capital of the kingdom.

The year 1896 marked the thousandth anniversary of the Magyar Conquest. The event was celebrated in sumptuous style, leaving permanent traces on the face of the capital (boulevards, Heroes' Square, City Park). Interest in 'Hungarianness' was intense. Architects struggled to invent a distinctively Hungarian way of building, in the process giving the international style of Art Nouveau (known here as Secession) a particular twist, and leaving a heritage of turn-of-the-century architecture unparalleled elsewhere in Europe. Hungary led the world in aspects of science and technology too: the electrical transformer was invented, and electricity applied to railway traction, on main lines as well as on the pioneering Budapest Metro, first of its kind in continental Europe.

There was a downside to this expansive era. The government in Budapest set out to

*Ornate Parliament*

thoroughly Magyarise its subjects, discouraging the use of any language other than Hungarian, closing down the cultural institutions of the minorities and making command of Hungarian the only avenue of advancement. Resentment of this was sufficient to undermine Budapest's authority at the end of World War I; caught on the losing side, Hungary was dismembered, its component nationalities splitting off to form parts of new or much expanded states.

**Trianon Hungary**

In 1920, the Hungarian government had no alternative but to sign the Treaty of Trianon. Imposed by the Allies, and bitterly resented ever since, this confirmed Hungary's new frontiers – but not before the shrunken state had undergone the revolutionary convulsions of Béla Kun's short-lived Soviet Republic (March to August 1919), and the counter-revolutionary White Terror instituted by Admiral Horthy, former chief of the Austro-Hungarian Navy. For the next quarter of a century the country was to be governed in an authoritarian manner by Horthy, who proclaimed himself regent in place of the deposed Habsburg King-Emperor Karl.

As the principal aim of Hungary's foreign policy was to recover its lost lands, the country was drawn even closer into the orbit of Nazi Germany. By Hitler's good graces, southern Slovakia was recovered in 1939, part of Transylvania in 1940, part of Yugoslavia in 1941. A Hungarian contingent set off, not altogether whole-heartedly, to help the Wehrmacht conquer the Soviet Union. In 1944, however, clumsy attempts to change sides in the lost war were countered by outright occupation by Germany; the Jews were rounded up for extermination by Adolf Eichmann, and a particularly gangsterish bunch of home-grown Nazis, the Arrow Cross, was installed as a puppet government. The country suffered grievously in the last months of the war, and Budapest in particular endured one of the greatest sieges of modern times, from late 1944 to early 1945, which left three-quarters of its buildings in ruins.

**Communist Hungary**

A provisional government had been set up in late 1944 in Debrecen, the first big city to be taken by the Red Army. This centre-left coalition was slowly subverted by the relatively small Communist Party. From 1948, Hungary found itself firmly to the east of the Iron Curtain, suffering all the miseries of Soviet-inspired totalitarianism: show trials and executions, expropriation of private property, censorship, suppression of religion, severance of all contacts with the West, Cold War hysteria and so on. Although the worst Stalinist excesses were over by the mid-1950s, Hungarians had had enough: in July 1956 the repulsive dictator Rákosi was finally ousted; in October student protests developed into open revolt. For a few short and delirious days the nation celebrated its freedom; under the benign leadership of the moderate Communist Imre Nagy. The new government declared itself neutral and called for the removal of Soviet forces from Hungarian soil. Pictures of teenagers with rifles attempting to defend the streets of Budapest against the columns of Russian tanks were seen in the media. Though strikes and protests continued until the end of the year, the Russian intervention spelled the end of this latest and most courageous of Hungarian uprisings. In the aftermath, hundreds of thousands fled the country, and Nagy and his associates were secretly tried, shot and buried.

Universal contempt was directed at the turncoat Communist leader János Kádár, who had initially supported the revolution but was then installed by the Soviets as puppet ruler. But Kádár was a paradoxical figure, and during the 32 years of his rule he saw to it that his country enjoyed maximum freedom within the Soviet straitjacket. A degree of private enterprise was tolerated, then encouraged. Hungary became the most outwardly prosperous (though heavily indebted) of all the Communist-ruled countries.

By the late 1980s, Kádár was finally made to resign. Efforts by the Party to reform were overtaken by the events of 1989. Border guards began to remove the barbed wire along the frontier with Austria, and the

*Magyars*

government refused to stop the Trabants and Wartburgs of East German tourists puttering westwards to freedom, acts which heralded the downfall of totalitarianism all over Eastern Europe.

**Hungary Now**

Since those heady days Hungary has become a multi-party state. At the elections of early 1990, the rule of the Communist Party came to an end, its successor in government being a centre-right coalition headed by the Hungarian Democratic Forum. The last Russian troops left in June 1991. Today's Hungary is in a bewildering state of rapid transformation. Hungarians, in the face of high inflation, are having to struggle harder than ever to make ends meet. Oppressive though it may have been, the Soviet Union represented a captive market for Hungarian industry, whose ability to adapt itself to a sophisticated and volatile world market is now being tested to (and in some cases, beyond) breaking point.

Hungarians face an uncertain but hopeful future, full of worries but convinced that there is no other way forward than to turn away from outdated creeds and take their place in a wider world.

**Landscapes and Townscapes**

Many of Hungary's landscapes link it to neighbouring countries, while others are utterly and uniquely Hungarian. Thus, while Hungary is by no means just an extension of Central Europe, the sub-Alpine hills and valleys of western Hungary and exquisite little towns like Köszeg are almost Austrian in character, and Central European influences are evident everywhere in the shape of fine baroque churches and mansions.

Until recent years, Hungary was very much a peasant country, with deep differences between rural and town life. It is the ambition of every flat-dweller to have a place in the country, and the proportion of second homes is one of the highest in Europe. Much of the countryside may consist of the featureless fields of former state farms, but on the outskirts of every settlement is a zone of 'closed gardens', a rich landscape of small plots of

*The carved stone of Matthias Church*

land growing vines, vegetables and fruit, each with its home-built chalet (or wine-cellar) providing a family retreat.

Though many village houses have been modernised, enough of the old rural architecture usually remains to make a stop worthwhile. There is also a surprisingly large number of 'skanzens' or open-air museums reflecting the great variety of local traditions in building (the largest and most fascinating of these is the national Museum of the Hungarian Village at Szentendre).

Hungarian towns are often a mixture of the familiar and the exotic. The onion-shaped domes of baroque churches are everywhere, contrasting strangely with the occasional mosque or minaret left over from Turkish times. At first glance, most main streets resemble their counterparts elsewhere, but closer inspection will often reveal features which are uniquely Hungarian. Prominent among them will be the turn-of-the-century civic buildings, apartments and office blocks in Secession style. Behind the main street, particularly in the towns of the Great Plain, city-scale buildings may soon give way to more modest structures, single-storey houses which seem to belong in the countryside rather than the town. And many such dwellings were indeed at one time the abode of country people who clustered together in the unsettled conditions of Turkish times in the relative security of town.

**Ethnic Variety**

Hungary was never an ethnically homogenous state. The Magyars may have ruled (often under a foreign king!), but the country's original far-flung boundaries included people of very varied origin – Slovaks, Germans, Croats, Serbs, Rumanians, as well as tribesmen allied to the Magyars, Cumanians, Pechenegs, and Palotians.

Germans in particular played an important role in the country's development, as marriage material for the mighty (like Stephen's Queen Gisela) or as the burghers and miners of the Middle Ages. Many of them were made to leave in the aftermath of World War II, but old-fashioned German dialects can still be heard in the countryside around Pécs, along the Austrian border or in the hills to the west of Budapest.

Serbs and other southern Slavs have also found sanctuary in Hungary, and something of their presence lives on in the icons and other fittings of the country's numerous Orthodox churches, such as Szentendre and Miskolc.

Jews have long lived in Hungary, but their numbers increased greatly in the 19th century, when a massive immigration took place from Poland and Russia. By the early 20th century Jews formed a quarter of the population of Budapest. Their wealth and prominence is reflected in the magnificent synagogues gracing many a town; the Great Synagogue in Budapest is particularly fine, and no visitor to Szeged should miss the outstanding New Synagogue.

*Frescos in Eger's Minorite Church*

The redrawing of the country's boundaries after World War I made Hungary ethnically much more 'pure', and today the great majority of the population can be considered to be ethnic Magyars. The largest minority is formed by the Gypsies, many of whom live in the northeast and are considered by some of their fellow citizens to be more troublesome than picturesque. Many Magyars are (somewhat reluctant) subjects of neighbouring countries. Transylvanian Hungarians of Romania are considered to be the guardians of particularly authentic forms of Magyardom, and their fate is observed with keen interest by the population of Hungary proper.

*Ráckeve Chateau*

# What to See

The Essential rating system:

✓ 'top ten'

◆◆◆ do not miss
◆◆ see if you can
◆ worth seeing if you have time

## BUDAPEST

Nature and history have combined to give this great Central European metropolis a unique personality. Budapest is not only one of the world's most beautiful capitals, with a long and unusually fascinating past, but a place of today, its intense cultural life having survived the long years of Communist rule and flourishing with renewed vigour in the freer but often confusing post-1989 climate.
The city is situated at the meeting point of the country's two great landscape types. It is here that the Danube finally frees itself from the embrace of the wooded hills, running southwest–northeast across the whole width of Hungary to flow along the western rim of the Great Plain. The uplands descend in stages to the Buda bank of the river, creating (in what has become Castle Hill) an easily fortified vantage point overlooking the river crossing. On the eastern bank, rising imperceptibly, the land stretches into the far distance, putting no constraints on the expansion of a great modern city.

Much of Budapest's beauty resides in its relationship to the great river. More than half a mile (0.9km) wide as it reaches the city at Margaret Island, the Danube narrows to a mere 750 feet (230m) as the great Gellert rock rears up on the west bank. From the promenade on the Pest side, the river offers a perfectly proportioned foreground for views of Castle Hill and the wooded heights beyond. Likewise, the views over the water from the ramparts of Buda or from the citadel crowning Gellert Hill cannot fail to rouse the enthusiasm of the most jaded sightseer.
In many ways Budapest is the tourist city par excellence, with an overall structure which can be easily grasped from any of the main viewpoints on hilltop or riverside. Buda's layout respects and enhances its hilly setting, while Pest on the eastern bank has a clear, man-made pattern of great boulevards which encircle its partly pedestrianised inner city and then radiate outwards. Terraces, promenades and squares seem to have been

designed for strolling and viewing at leisure. The harmony of the scene is completed by the fine bridges linking the two parts of the great city.

For centuries, however, the Danube separated, rather than joined, Buda on the west bank with Pest on the east. Together with Óbuda (Old Buda), the ancestor of them both, they were only formed into a single unit in 1873. Even then, each part retained its own personality, Buda being older, staider, conscious of its long history, Pest being brasher, go-ahead, looking to the future. This latter part of the 19th century was the city's Golden Age, the time when it grew faster than most European cities to become the great capital of what was then a great kingdom stretching from the Adriatic to the Carpathians. Today's Budapest, with its more than 2 million inhabitants, is still a great city. All roads lead here, and no provincial city comes anywhere near to challenging its pre-eminence in every field.

Like the country as a whole, Budapest's history has not been a happy one, destruction and suppression being recurring themes. The Mongols laid the place waste in 1241–2 and the long siege which finally freed the city from Turkish rule in 1686 had much the same effect. One national revolution was put down bloodily in 1849 by Austrians and Russians, and in November 1956, the city's streets were streaked with blood as the Red Army's tanks squashed another attempt by the citizens of the capital to free their land from foreign domination. Before this, in the last winter of World War II, much of the city had been levelled as the besieged German Wehrmacht and their Hungarian hangers-on offered a desperate

*The illuminated Chain Bridge*

resistance to the Red Army. But rebuilding has always followed destruction; Budapest's brilliant baroque heritage came about through the need to make good the damage sustained during the struggle to drive out the Turks, and in few cities have the wounds of World War II been so impeccably healed as here. Budapest managed to keep at least something of its special allure during the interminable decades of Communist rule. The economic liberalisation of the 1960s, together perhaps with a deep-seated Hungarian reluctance to forgo some of the better things of life, led to a greater liveliness in the street scene than in any other capital of the Communist world. Cafés, shops, kiosks, florists, vendors of fruit and vegetables – all flourished here as nowhere else east of the Iron Curtain. This animation is all the more intense today as the capital's inhabitants adjust themselves to the sometimes bewildering opportunities of the post-1989 situation. A new spirit of enterprise manifests itself not only in glossy shopfronts and expensive restaurants, but also in sandwichboard men advertising dubious delights, in hucksters and hustlers, and graffiti artists.

**Places of Interest**
The main sites are grouped alphabetically under four headings: **Buda** (page 21), **Pest** (page 26), **Outer Budapest** (page 30) and **Excursions**, which also includes the Lake Balaton area (page 37).

**Buda (Castle Hill)**
Most visitors will begin their exploration high up here in the ancient core of the city with its wealth of historic buildings and incomparable panorama over the Danube. Cars are restricted, so the best way up is either on foot via the steps and paths lacing the slopes of the hill, by shuttle bus from Moszkva tér metro station or, more entertainingly, by the Sikló, the recently restored cable railway.

Duna (The Danube)
More than any other city along its banks, Budapest turns its face to the Danube, lining it with promenades and spanning it with superb bridges. One of the best ways to experience the city is from the deck of the pleasure boats which ply from the Pest quay, mingling with barge traffic bound for Black Sea or Rhine. Eight bridges link Buda with Pest. The three central ones come constantly into view as one moves about the city. The stately Széchenyi Chain Bridge (Lánc-híd) was the first to be built, in 1849. Downstream stands the elegant Elizabeth Bridge (Erzsébet-híd), named after the Hungarians' favourite Habsburg, Franz Josef's queen. Last of this central trio is the Freedom Bridge (Szabadság-híd), opened for the Millennial celebrations in 1896. Its highly decorative metalwork is topped by the mythical turul bird and the nation's coat of arms.

◆◆◆
## BUDAVÁRI PALOTA (THE ROYAL PALACE) ✓

This huge edifice with its immensely long façade (some 1,000ft/300m) glowers down on the Danube and completely dominates the southern end of Castle Hill. Its commanding presence seems all that a royal palace should be, yet what we see today is relatively new and was never really lived in by Hungary's absentee Habsburg rulers. It now serves as an admirable home to several of the capital's museums.

Next to the glass pavilion housing the station of the Sikló are the splendid railings, gateway and steps giving access to the esplanade in front of the palace. You can get your bearings by the swaggering statue of Eugene of Savoy on horseback. Far below, the Danube; above, the colonnade and dome of the palace, rising high over the rooms containing the collection of the **Magyar Nemzeti Galéria** (National Gallery). This is the storehouse of Hungarian art, of interest even to the casual visitor from abroad. Much space is occupied by 19th-century historical paintings. Stunning medieval carving, the visionary landscapes of the Pécs painter Csontváry, and the fresh outdoors as painted by turn-of-the-century artists like Károly Ferenczy can also be seen.

The present palace is built over the ruins of its predecessor, destroyed during the long

*The Royal Palace, largely reconstructed after World War II*

siege which brought Turkish rule to an end in 1686. Enough has been preserved deep below today's ground level to evoke the atmosphere of medieval times (statues of foppish courtiers in the Gothic hall) and the Renaissance splendours of King Matthias' reign. Echoes of courtly life linger in the gardens below the **Budapesti Történeti Múzeum** (Budapest History Museum), while the walls, towers and bastions beyond remind us that this was a fortress as well as a palace.

The western wing overlooking the palace's vast cobbled courtyard contains the **National Library**, named after Count Széchenyi. Beyond the great archway is another courtyard, open to the west, whose most intriguing feature is the 1904 **Matthias Well**, which shows the proud king as a huntsman. The northern wing of the palace houses the **Modern History Museum** and the **Ludwig Collection** of contemporary art.

◆◆◆

### GELLÉRT-HEGY (GELLERT HILL)

Few capitals can claim a cliff in their midst like this one. Named after the 11th-century saint who was martyred by being pushed over the edge (aboard a wheelbarrow, according to one account, nailed into a barrel according to another), it plunges precipitously into the waters of the Danube, forcing the river into the narrowest section of its bed.

St Gellért's statue, backed by a colonnade, stands a little way up the hill. The pathway continues to the top, though most prefer the road approach from the far side. Steps lead to a romantic path up through the trees, with the occasional vertiginous view of river and city.

The summit is largely occupied by the sprawling fortress known as the **Citadella**, built after the unsuccessful 1848 revolution to cow the mutinous populace. It now houses a hostel, restaurant and wine-cellar. With its giant female figure holding aloft a palm leaf, the **Liberation Monument** just below the citadel commemorates the freeing of Budapest from Nazi rule in 1945.

The views all around are superb. At the foot of the gentler wooded southern slopes of the hill stands the **Gellért Hotel** and **Spa** (see also page 34). A massive presence in pale stone, this internationally renowned establishment almost looks like an extension of the crags from which St Gellért was so rudely thrust. The façades of this great monument of Art Nouveau are remarkable enough, but the thermal baths, fed by one of Budapest's many springs, are truly spectacular. The galleried main pool could be the setting for an aquatic production of Mozart's *Magic Flute*, while the multi-coloured encrustations of the Turkish baths almost beggar description. Hotel guests descend to these delights in a private lift, but all the facilities are open to the public (including outdoor pools) and beg to be experienced.

### ◆◆◆ HALÁSZBASTYA (FISHERMEN'S BASTION) ✓

The country's first Christian king, Stephen, his saintliness confirmed by halo and cross, sits on his horse at the foot of the slope leading down from the Matthias Church to Buda's great belvedere, the Fishermen's Bastion.
Designed by Frigyes Schulek, and built around 1903 to coincide with the city's 1,000th anniversary celebrations, it was named after the old fish market which once flourished near by. The bastion, in white limestone, is an extraordinary effusion of towers, steps and viewing terraces; it twists its way along the top of the old walls towards the **Hilton Hotel**. This too is one of the city's sights, a bulky building, cleverly incorporating within its glass walls the remains of a Dominican church.

### ◆◆◆ MÁTYÁS-TEMPLOM (MATTHIAS CHURCH)

From the Royal Palace, the ramparts run northward, giving marvellous views over the river to Pest, and join Tárnok utca which channels the stream of tourists towards Szentháromság tér (Trinity Square) past souvenir sellers, street musicians and droshky drivers. The square is overlooked by Matthias Church, its 263 foot-high (80m) spire acting as a beacon all over the city. Officially dedicated to Our Lady, the church was founded in the 13th century and rebuilt in the 14th. The Turks made it into a mosque, removing the

furnishings and white-washing the walls. On their withdrawal the church was thoroughly and sumptuously baroquified. Its most comprehensive remodelling, however, dates from a century ago, when architects' enthusiasm for the Gothic knew no bounds. The result, inside as well as out, is a spectacular demonstration of Victorian virtuosity, more medieval than the Middle Ages. The church's associations with Hungary's rulers are many: early kings would present themselves here after their coronation at Székesfehervár, King Matthias was wed here (twice!) and crowned too. Franz Josef was crowned king of Hungary here in 1867, as was his ill-fated nephew Karl, in 1916.

*The neo-Romanesque Fishermen's Bastion provides spectacular views of the city*

### OLD STREETS OF BUDA

Once the commotion around Trinity Square (Szentháromság tér) has been left behind, Buda exhales the atmosphere of a tranquil country town. Its quiet streets are lined with modest burghers' dwellings, whose 18th- and 19th- century façades often belie much earlier origins, evidence of which is provided by the numerous medieval arched niches to be glimpsed in entrance ways.

The counterpart to the Fishermen's Bastion overlooking Pest is the long **rampart walk** on the far side of the hill. This gives fine views over the lower parts of Buda and of the smarter suburbs. In Kapisztrán tér stands a great octagonal stump of a tower, a poignant reminder of the destruction wrought in 1945, and all that is left of the Magdalen Church apart from foundations and a single window.

On the rampart, an array of retired weaponry guards the entrance to a former barracks, now the **Hadtörténeti Múzeum** (Military History Museum). With fine displays of arms and uniforms, pictures and proclamations, this tells the story of the glorious – but on the whole not very effective – feats of the Hungarian army. Around the corner from the museum is a touching tribute to the Turkish governor of Buda who fell in the siege of 1686.

**Pest**

The inner city of Pest is tightly defined by the ring of boulevards (known as the Little Boulevard – Kiskörút) running along the line of the old city walls from the Chain Bridge to Freedom Bridge. This area is sliced neatly into two by another boulevard, Kossuth Lajos utca. The southern half is workaday, the northern half 'smart', but both have the feel of an old city, with buildings facing each other across narrow streets and irregularly shaped squares. Between the Little Boulevard and the outer 'Great' Boulevard (Nagykörút) stretches the vast rectilinear city designed on the drawing boards of the 19th-century planners, with its long vistas, monumental public buildings and uniform apartment blocks, very reminiscent of the Paris of the same epoch.

◆

## BAZILIKA – SZENT ISTVÁN (ST STEPHEN'S CHURCH)

Just to the north of Erzsébet tér looms the great bulk of St Stephen's Basilica, turning its colonnaded apse to the boulevard and its principal façade to the square. This is the city's biggest church, built (with some difficulty – the dome collapsed during construction) between 1851 and 1905 to rival the great new cathedrals at Esztergom and Eger. It can house a congregation of several thousand worshippers and its dome tops 315 feet (96m). In a side chapel is one of Hungary's most precious relics, the preserved hand of St Stephen.

◆◆◆

## BELGRÁD RAKPART (DANUBE PROMENADE) ✓

Roman ruins have to fight hard to compete with the superb panorama of Buda on the far side of the river, and few city strolls can match the sheer visual pleasure of the promenade between Elizabeth Bridge and Chain Bridge. At the turn of the century this was the Korzo, the place to see and be seen. The old terrace cafés and hotels have gone, replaced by modern and somewhat faceless counterparts, but the trams still glide above the quayside and the promenade itself has been attractively paved and planted. Set back behind the square with the red marble obelisk commemorating the Russian dead of 1945, is the mid-19th-century concert hall known as the **Vigadó**, the extraordinarily romantic interior of which you should certainly try to see. Another interior which is one of the sights of the city is that of the **Hyatt Hotel**, from whose airy atrium hangs a replica of the first Hungarian aircraft. Most of Pest's share of the capital's many monuments and museums is to be found along the **Little Boulevard** or a short way beyond **Roosevelt tér**. Apart from the cluster of attractions around Heroes' Square, it is quite feasible to do your visiting in a leisurely way on foot. This will give you the chance to absorb atmosphere and take in the detail of Art Nouveau (or occasional post-modern) façades and the life of inner courtyards.

*Every bridge over the Danube at Budapest was destroyed during World War ll. Elizabeth Bridge, however, was unique in being the only one rebuilt to a new design*

◆◆

### IPARMÜVÉSZETI MÚZEUM (APPLIED ARTS MUSEUM)

At Kálvin tér the Little Boulevard is joined by Üllüi út. Two blocks along near the junction with the Great Boulevard, and worth the walk even if you do not go inside (but do!), is the extraordinary Art Nouveau palace built to house the collections of the Iparmüvészeti Múzeum. The visual confusion engendered by its weird forms, clad in clashing coloured tiles, can be relieved by contemplating the cool white and spacious interior, with its gorgeous array of antique furniture and decorative objects of all kinds, including a metal filigree figure of Napoleon.

◆

### KÖZPONTI VÁSÁRCSARNOK (CENTRAL MARKET HALL)

Budapest has a number of market halls, built around the turn of the century and looking very much alike. The biggest and liveliest, with lots of very organic-looking produce on display under its splendid roof, is on the final stretch of the Little Boulevard as it heads for the Freedom Bridge (Szabadság-híd).

◆

### NAGYZSINAGÓGA (GREAT SYNAGOGUE)

A temple of a very different kind from the Basilica is to be found just off Károly körút, part of the Little Boulevard. Before the Nazis came in 1944, Budapest's Jewish community was one of the largest in Europe, its wealth and importance reflected by the Great Synagogue which dominates the junction of Wesselényi and Dohány Streets. With its twin onion-shaped domes, this exotic edifice was built in the 1850s in a striking blend of Moorish and Byzantine styles. **Zsidó Múzeum** (Jewish Museum) documents the mixed fortunes of Hungarian Jewry, and there is a striking Holocaust Memorial.

◆◆
### NEMZETI MÚZEUM (NATIONAL MUSEUM)

The Old Astoria Hotel gives its name to the crossing of Rákóczi út/Kossuth Lajos utca with the Little Boulevard, which here becomes Múzeum körút. And indeed it is here, standing back from the ceaseless flow of traffic in its own little park, that one of Hungary's most prestigious museums is to be found, the Magyar Nemzeti Múzeum. This was completed in 1847, just in time for its grandiose steps and great Grecian portico to lend credibility to the revolutionaries who harangued the crowds here in March 1848. The most fascinating historical relics are probably those gathered together to chronicle the country's history from the Conquest in AD896 to the defeat of the national uprising in 1849. Among the rich array of evocative objects (arms and armour, portraits, models, furniture, jewellery, costumes) the most surprising is the luxuriously fitted-out Turkish tent, captured from its commander at the siege of Vienna in 1683. The Hungarian Crown Jewels are displayed in a separate section.

**The Hungarian Crown Jewels**
Though the country is no longer a kingdom, its coronation regalia are still revered as the supreme symbols of statehood. They consist of orb and sceptre, cloak and sword, and above all the unique crown named after King Stephen. This is not in fact the crown placed on the saintly monarch's head by Pope Sylvester in AD1000, but a two-part, composite creation; the 'Greek crown', an 11th-century golden head-band richly ornamented with jewels, enamels and pendants, and the 'Latin crown' of somewhat later date, topped by the hastily mounted crooked crown of 1551. It last sat on the head of a king of Hungary when Karl of Habsburg was crowned in Buda in 1916.
The crown has suffered many fates over the centuries, having been hidden, stolen, spirited away and bought and sold. Its most recent adventure was at the end of World War II, when it was taken to Vienna by the fleeing Hungarian collaborators with the Nazis. Subsequently impounded by the Americans in Fort Knox, it finally returned home in 1978.

◆
### NÉPRAJZI MÚZEUM (ETHNOGRAPHICAL MUSEUM)

The gloomy expanse of tarmac on the landward side of Parliament, with its conifer trees and statues (Kossuth to the north, Rákóczi to the south), is bounded by a neo-Renaissance palace housing the collections of the Ethnographical Museum. The pomp and circumstance of the interior almost outbid the exhibits which are nevertheless excellent, a fine introduction to the country's wonderfully rich folklore.

◆◆
### ORSZÁGHÁZ (PARLIAMENT BUILDING)

On a prime riverside site to the north of Roosevelt tér stands the city's most impressive edifice, the almost incredibly romantic Parliament Building. Perhaps best seen from the far bank of the Danube, this gothic dream of spires and spikes, turrets and pinnacles clustering around the great central dome (topped for 40 years by a red star) was completed in the heyday of Hungarian confidence, a palace for parliamentarians who governed a country three times its present size. It architect, Imre Steindle, died a few weeks before its completion in 1902. Group tours of the breathtaking interior can be arranged (tel: 112 0600).

◆◆◆
### VÁCI UTCA (VÁC STREET)

Pedestrianised like Vörösmarty Square and even more crowded, the city's prime shopping street winds its way southwards past elegant stores, cafés, restaurants and bookshops. At **Ferenciek tér** (Franciscan's Square) is the point of greatest animation, as passengers cram themselves into the blue city buses to cross the river, and shoppers swarm around the highly decorated **Párizsi Udvar** (Paris Arcade). Beyond the tall twin buildings guarding the bridge approach is the solemn baroque façade of the **Belvárosi plébánia-templom** (Inner City Parish Church) and, next to it, the remains of the Roman foothold of this bank of the Danube, **Contra Aquincum**.

◆◆◆
### VÖRÖSMARTY TÉR (VÖRÖSMARTY SQUARE)

This is the place to meet friends or start exploring Inner Pest. Normally thronged with shoppers, tourists, buskers and those with time on their hands, the square focuses on the memorial to the patriotic 19th-century poet Mihály Vörösmarty. A large and superior record store occupies part of one building, while **Gerbeaud's**, the extremely high-class patisserie (see page 36), spreads over several, and makes a good all-weather rendezvous.

*Vörösmarty memorial statue*

**Outer Budapest**

The sheer extent of the great 19th-century city makes it sensible to undertake part of your exploration on the excellent public transport system. The Metro is a useful aid here. It runs from the centre to all the main line railway stations, two of which (Keleti and Nyugati, east and west) are constructed of glass and metal, well worth a visit in their own right. The first metro line was built in 1896 (part of it is preserved as a museum piece off the Deák tér underpass) to speed visitors to the Millennial celebrations. It still runs from the inner city, underneath the surface of ruler-straight Andrássy út, to the cluster of monuments around the entrance to Budapest's biggest and most popular park, the Városliget (City Forest).

◆

ANDRÁSSY ÚT (ANDRÁSSY STREET)

A mile-and-a-half (2.5km) long, Andrássy út (also known as Népköztárs-asag utja) was laid out in anticipation of the Millennial festival. It begins as a conventional boulevard, gradually acquiring more greenery as continuous city façades give way to villas. Along the way it passes the **State Opera House** (centre of the theatre district) and the important junctions known as the **Oktogon** and the **Kodály körönd** (Kodály Circus). But the culmination of the route is unquestionably Heroes' Square, focal point of the 1896 spectacular marking a thousand years of Hungarian statehood.

*The colonnade in Heroes' Square*

◆

BATTHYÁNY TÉR (BATTHYÁNY SQUARE)

Conveniently situated on the metro line linking Moszkva tér with the centre of Pest, this square in Buda offers one of the best views of the Parliament Building on the far side of the Danube. The local church, dedicated to St Anne, is one of the city's most pleasing baroque buildings, impressive enough on the outside with its twin towers, but charmingly intimate within. Its parish hall is now one of Budapest's most delightful cafés. Casanova is supposed to have stayed at the **White Cross Inn** on the west side of the square. Along Fö utca to the north is the city's best-preserved Turkish bath, known as **Király fürdö** (King's Baths). Much added to, topped by its Turkish crescent and still in use, it has kept its strange domes and complements the little **Church of St Florian** which faces it across the tiny park.

◆◆◆
## HÖSÖK TERE (HEROES' SQUARE) ✓

This huge space absorbs its swarms of visitors and their coaches with consummate ease. From its centre rises the **Millenary Monument**. Around the base of its tall column are grouped the seven chieftans, Árpád among them, who led their tribes into Hungary in 896. Their expressions are fierce, befitting ruthless conquerors, their apparel (stag-horn helmets) intimidating. From their midst rises a tall column with the archangel Gabriel bearing the Apostolic cross and the Hungarian crown. The colonnade in the background houses a further array of heroes. The square is flanked by two galleries, one major, one (relatively) minor. The **Mücsarnok** is used for temporary exhibitions, while the vast Szépmüveszeti Múzeum (see separate entry) has one of the world's great art collections.

◆◆
## MARGIT-SZIGET (MARGARET ISLAND)

The Danube is one of those rivers which sometimes seems undecided about how to find its way. In the course of its journey to the Black Sea it often tries alternatives, its branches forming islands, some of them recognisable as such, some of them, like Csepel-sziget (Island) just south of Budapest, so long they almost form little continents. Margaret Island is given over entirely to relaxation and recreation, being perhaps the finest park in the city. Popular though it is, its location seems to lend it a special air of refinement, allowing visitors to reminisce about the monks and nuns who previously dwelt here in seclusion. Among them was the daughter of King Béla IV, Princess Margaret, after whom the place is named. The ruins of her nunnery can still be seen, just to the èast of the impressive water-tower.
The island is big enough to hide its many facilities (swimming pools – with artificial waves! – a tennis stadium, open-air theatre, casino, cafés and hotels) among the generous green of its trees and gardens. Its tranquillity is helped by the exclusion of cars, which are only admitted from the modern Árpád Bridge to the north, and then only to the car-parks clustering around the two hotels at this end of the island. The famous Grand (now the Ramada Grand) Hotel has recently been modernised, while the Thermal Hotel was built over a spring discovered in the 19th century.

◆◆◆
## SZÉPMÜVÉSZETI MÚZEUM (FINE ARTS MUSEUM)

*Heroes' Square*

The treasures of this major museum, housed in its splendid Grecian temple, range from Egyptian antiquities to modern sculpture. The core consists of a vast number of Old Masters (including Raphael, Rembrandt, Brueghel, Holbein, Vermeer, Velasquez and Goya) and fine 19th-century works (Manet,

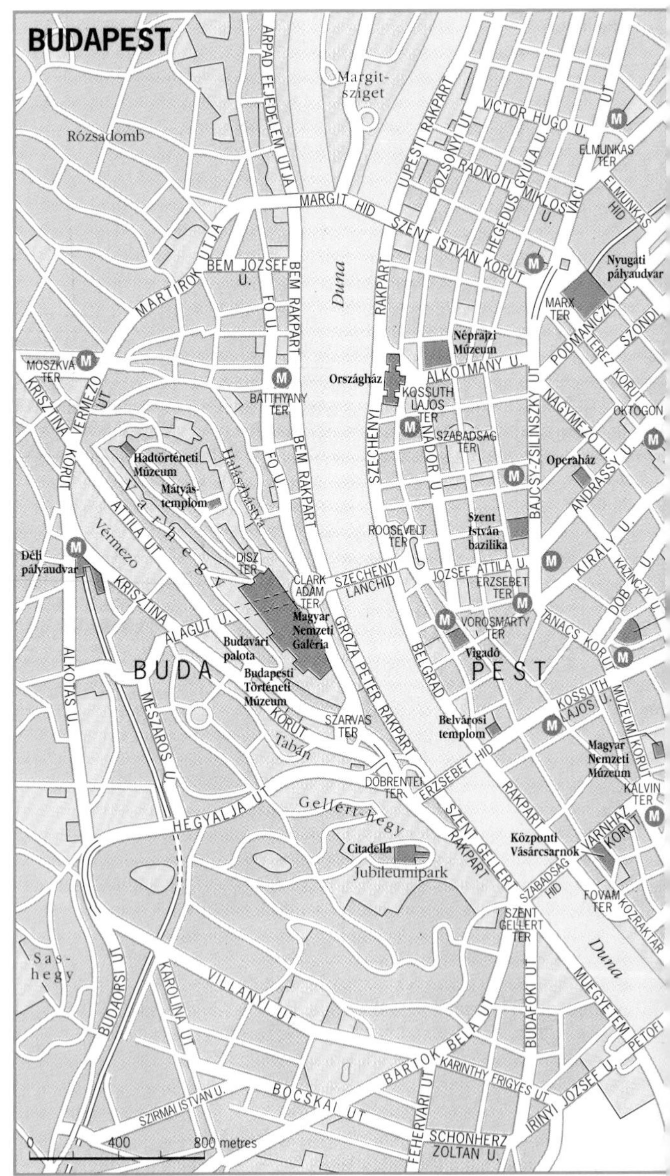
BUDAPEST
Margit-sziget
Rózsadomb
ÁRPÁD FEJEDELEM ÚTJA
MARGIT HÍD
SZENT ISTVÁN KÖRÚT
VICTOR HUGO U.
ÚJPESTI RAKPART
POZSONYI ÚT
RADNÓTI MIKLÓS U.
GYULA U.
HEGEDŰS
VÁCI ÚT
ELMUNKÁS TÉR
ELMUNKÁS HÍD
Nyugati pályaudvar
MARX TÉR
PODMANICZKY U.
SZONDI
TERÉZ KÖRÚT
MARTIROK ÚTJA
BEM JÓZSEF U.
FŐ U.
BEM RAKPART
Duna
RAKPART
Néprajzi Múzeum
ALKOTMÁNY U.
Országház
KOSSUTH LAJOS TÉR
SZABADSÁG TÉR
NÁDOR U.
BAJCSY-ZSILINSZKY ÚT
NAGYMEZŐ U.
OKTOGON
Operaház
ANDRÁSSY ÚT
MOSZKVA TÉR
KRISZTINA KÖRÚT
VÉRMEZŐ ÚT
BATTHYÁNY TÉR
Hadtörténeti Múzeum
Halászbástya
Mátyás-templom
Várhegy
SZÉCHENYI RAKPART
Vérmező
ATTILA ÚT
Szent István bazilika
ROOSEVELT TÉR
Déli pályaudvar
DÍSZ TÉR
CLARK ÁDÁM TÉR
SZÉCHENYI LÁNCHÍD
JÓZSEF ATTILA U.
ERZSÉBET TÉR
KIRÁLY U.
KAZINCZY U.
DOB U.
KRISZTINA
ALAGÚT U.
Magyar Nemzeti Galéria
Budavári palota
GRÓZA PÉTER RAKPART
VÖRÖSMARTY TÉR
Vigadó
TANÁCS KÖRÚT
BUDA
PEST
BELGRÁD
Budapesti Történeti Múzeum
ALKOTÁS U.
MÉSZÁROS U.
KÖRÚT
SZARVAS TÉR
Tabán
Belvárosi templom
KOSSUTH LAJOS U.
MÚZEUM KÖRÚT
Magyar Nemzeti Múzeum
ERZSÉBET HÍD
DOBRENTEI TÉR
RAKPART
KÁLVIN TÉR
Gellért-hegy
HEGYALJA ÚT
SZENT GELLÉRT RAKPART
Központi Vásárcsarnok
VÁRNHÁZ KÖRÚT
Citadella
Jubileumipark
SZABADSÁG HÍD
FŐVÁM TÉR
KÖZRAKTÁR
SZENT GELLÉRT TÉR
Duna
Sas-hegy
BUDAÖRSI ÚT
KAROLINA ÚT
VILLÁNYI ÚT
BUDAFOKI ÚT
MŰEGYETEM
BARTÓK BÉLA ÚT
PETŐFI
KARINTHY FRIGYES ÚT
IRINYI JÓZSEF U.
BOCSKAI ÚT
SZIRMAI ISTVÁN U.
FEHÉRVÁRI ÚT
SCHÖNHERZ ZOLTÁN U.
0
400
800 metres

Monet, Cezanne, Gauguin), enough to detain you for a day.

◆

## VÁROSLIGET (CITY PARK)

Above the trees of the City Park rises the romantic silhouette of **Vajdahunyad vára** (Castle). This is a Disneyland creation before Disney, a playful assemblage of all the country's architectural styles, intended as a backdrop to the 1896 Expo, but enjoyed so much that it was preserved when the celebrations came to an end. Further features draw the crowds into the park, like the **zoo** with its elephant gates, **Gundel's** famous restaurant, the **Vidám** (Amusement) Park, the **Közlekedési Múzeum** (Transport Museum), the **Széchenyi gyógyfürdö** (Baths) with their Art Nouveau mosaic, and **Petőfi Csarnok**, the metropolitan youth centre and 'stronghold of Hungarian rock and roll' (András Török).

## Practical Budapest

### Accommodation

Book early for Budapest – the city has plenty of hotels but even more visitors! Life is easier if you are rich; 4–5-star hotels are relatively numerous and some of them count as tourist attractions in their own right. Moving lower down the scale may give you less choice of location, and you should always check where your accommodation is in relation to public transport. A shortage of cheaper hotels is compensated for by an abundance of private rooms. Try **Ibusz**, Petőfi tér 3 (behind the Intercontinental Hotel), tel: 181 1453.

**Hilton**, Hess András tér 1–3 (tel: 175 1000), 5-star. This suave and elegant hotel in old Buda incorporates the remains of a cloister, Dominican church and medieval tower. The rooms overlooking the Fishermen's Bastion enjoy some of the best views of the city. Given its lounges, coffee shop and the first-rate Kalocsa Restaurant, you could spend your entire holiday here. Expensive, but still less so than its equivalents in the West.

**Gellért**, Gellért tér 1 (tel: 185 2200), 4-star. One of Budapest's landmarks at the Buda end of the Szabadság-híd (Freedom Bridge), the last of the great riverside grand hotels. Guests have the use of a private lift to the wonderful baths and pools of the spa which forms part of the hotel. Danube Restaurant with international cuisine, Gellért brasserie and Espresso Café.

**Forum** , Apáczai Csere János 12–14 (tel: 117 8088), 4-star. Impeccable service combined with a prime site on the Danube Promenade make this a favourite among the city's luxury hotels. The rooms facing the river have incomparable views of Castle Hill.

**Ramada Grand Hotel**, Margitsziget (tel: 111 1000), 4-star. Luxuriously restored old hotel at the tranquil northern tip of Margaret Island. Elegant restaurant with international specialities and attractive open-air terrace in summer, plus brasserie serving the famous Austrian Gösser beer.

**Astoria**, Kossuth Lu 19 (tel: 117 3411), 3-star. An old-established place, recently restored to former glory, in the centre of Pest. The Hungarian Revolution was proclaimed here on the last day of October 1918. Restaurant and bar with dance-band and show.

**Taverna**, Váci u 20 (tel: 138 4999), 3-star. Large modern (or rather, post-modern) building in the city's premier shopping street. Bar, fast-food restaurant, German-style beer cellar.

**Wien**, Budaörsi út 88 - 90 (tel: 166 5400), 2-star. Not very atmospheric, but a convenient location on the approach to the motorway leading westward to Balaton and Vienna (Wien).

**Citadella**, Citadella sétány (tel: 166 5794),1-star. Limited accommodation fitted into the Habsburg fortress on the top of Gellért Hill. The restaurant is more atmospheric than gastronomic.

For a selection of moderately priced accommodation you could try the range of 2-star hotels managed by Eravis (1113 Budapest, Bartók Béla út 152, tel: 185 1188). The personnel, if not yet expert, are likely to be trying hard. One such place is: **Hotel Ventura**, Fehérvári út 179 (tel: 181 0758). A faceless block a fair distance from the centre in the southern Kelenfold suburb, but trams will bear you swiftly and directly to the foot of Castle Hill and the centre of Pest.

Young people are catered for by the **Express Travel Agency** at Semmelweiss utca 4 (tel: 117 6634), and at the **Keleti** (East) **Station**. They have access to youth hostels and, during parts of the academic vacations, to university halls of residence.

## Eating Out

### Restaurants

As only to be expected in the capital of a nation of food lovers, Budapest has any number of places to eat. If expense is no problem, join the other visitors from abroad and the local *nouveaux-riches* enjoying Hungarian and international specialities in any of the restaurants attached to the big hotels (see above, and also the **Csárda** in the Duna Intercontinental and the **Old Timer** in the Atrium Hyatt, both with views over the Danube to Castle Hill). Gypsy music will accompany your meal in most cases.

*Al fresco at Gundel's restaurant*

#### Pest

**Gundel**, Állatkerti körút 2 (tel: 12 21 002), is one of the city's old established (founded in 1896) and famous restaurants, situated on the edge of the Városliget (City Forest). Lavishly restored and serving international and Hungarian dishes, including their own renowned pancake.

**Apostolok**, Kigyó u 4–6 (tel: 11 83 704). In the heart of the pedestrianised shopping area near Váci utca. Strudels are a speciality of this atmospheric brasserie. A less atmospheric but reliable brasserie with a Germanic ambience is in the basement of the Taverna Hotel just round the corner in Váci utca itself (no 20, tel: 13 84 999).

**Hungária**, Terez körút 9–11 (tel: 12 23 849). The old New York Café on the Big Boulevard was built at the end of the 19th century, becoming an intellectuals' café, where philosophers argued, writers scribbled, music was composed and newspapers were read. The decor is sumptuous, the cuisine international.

**Szindbád**, Markó u 33 (tel: 13 22 966). This cellar restaurant excels in famous specialities and impeccable service. Beef-marrow on toast is an all too filling starter, and main courses are guaranteed to give satisfaction. Highly rated.

#### Buda

The restaurants on Castle Hill are inevitably geared to the needs of tourists. The **Arany Hordó**, Tárnok u 16 (tel: 15 61 367) is housed in a restored medieval building full of atmosphere, and consists of a restaurant, brasserie and wine-cellar, which resembles a grotto. The equally atmospheric **Régi Országház**, Országház, u 17 (tel: 17 51 767), also with wine-cellar, has a garden

restaurant in summer. Lacking the gypsy music offered in both the above, the **Fekete Holló**, Országház u 10 (tel: 156 0175), offers the best value for money on the hill.
Below Castle Hill are two contrasting restaurants. The **Tabáni kakas**, Attila út 27 (tel: 175 7165) is just to the south, in the Tabán district, serving good typical food (eg smoked pork and beans) together with some international dishes at very reasonable prices. Equally good food, served in a much more sophisticated ambience, and correspondingly rather more expensive, is available in the Víziváros (Watertown) area to the north, at the **Kacsa**, Fö u 75 (tel: 135 3357).

*Highly decorative State Opera*

**Óbuda**
A cluster of restaurants, most of them serving fish specialities, occupy the buildings around the old square which is all that is left of the ancient settlement of Óbuda (Old Buda). The **Sipos Halászkert**, Fö tér 6 (tel: 188 8745) is a cheerful, bustling place, used to dealing with foreigners in quantity. Freshwater fish in its many forms (such as the famous *fogas*) is what must be tried here, though many other dishes are available.

### Cafés and patisseries

**Gerbeaud**, Vörösmarty tér 7 (tel: 11 81 311). The most famous establishment of its kind, founded in the mid-19th century. Furnished in period style, its location at the epicentre of city life – as well as its cakes – make it a favourite stop for residents and tourists alike.
Both in Andrássy út, but several blocks from each other, are **Müvész**, no 29 (tel: 12 24 606) and **Lukács**, no 70 (tel: 13 21 371); the historic decor of both enjoys statutory protection.
**Ruszwurm**, Szentháromság u 3 (tel: 17 55 284), has been serving its cakes to ever increasing crowds on Castle Hill since the early 19th century. Intimate Biedermeier interior.
**Angelika**, Batthyány tér 7 (tel: 11 55 233). Probably the most comfortable of the capital's cafés, housed in the old parish centre of St Anne's Church.

### Entertainment
The German/English *Programme in Ungarn/in Hungary* provides lots of detail.

Given the inaccessibility of the Hungarian language, and bearing in mind the country's fine musical traditions, opera and concerts are perhaps a better bet than theatre, though cinemas show many films in the original version.

There are two opera houses, the splendid **State Opera** in Andrássy út and the more 'popular' **Erkel Theatre** in Köztársaság tér. The latter tends to put on vigorous performances of epic historical operas. The most prestigious concerts are those held at the **Zeneakadémia** (Academy of Music) on the corner of Király utca and Liszt Ferenc tér, and in the spectacular auditorium of the **Vigadó** just off the Danube Promenade. Tickets can be bought at the ticket office at 1 Vörösmarty tér (or possibly at your hotel).

Jazz and rock command a considerable following. The Benkö Dixieland Band and the Hobo Blues Band are both internationally famous. The **Petőfi Csarnok** in the City Forest accommodates the young crowd at its discos and open-air concerts.

Folklore performances are put on at the **Fövárosi Müvelödési Ház,** Fehérvári út 47 (tel: 181 1360), and in the so-called Dance Houses (*Táncházak*).

Nightclubs exist in most of the grander hotels, catering mostly for tourists. Others express their aspirations with names like **Maxim Varieté** and **Moulin Rouge.** The **Casanova** in Battyány tér is perhaps more original. There are four casinos in all, one on a Danube steamer.

# AROUND BUDAPEST

## Excursions from Budapest

◆

### BUDA HILLS (BUDAI HEGYSÉG)

When city stress and traffic fumes become intolerable, those Budapesters who can head for the cleaner air filtered by the fine beech woods on these limestone heights, west of the city. The best way up to the top is on the rack and pinion railway, whose lower terminus is a brisk walk or short tram ride from the

Moszkva tér metro station. This climbs steeply through the leafy suburbs and deposits you on Széchenyi-hegy (Széchenyi Hill), near Pioneer Railway terminus, which, staffed by children, runs for several miles through the forest.

The highest point of the Buda Hills, at 1736 feet (529m), is János-hegy, a not-too-arduous walk up from the Pioneer railway station of the same name. The summit is crowned by an elaborate viewing tower, built by the architect of the Fishermen's Bastion; the views from the top are spectacular.

◆

### CSEPEL ISLAND (CSEPEL-SZIGET)

Csepel Island stretches 34 miles (54km) downstream, from Budapest. The calm waters of the eastern arm of the Danube (Soroksári Duna) have long been a favourite place for city folk to spend their weekends messing about in boats.

**Ráckeve**, the terminus of the suburban railway towards the southern end of the island, was one of many places founded by Serbs fleeing northwards from the Turks. The Greek Orthodox Church is unusual in that it was begun as early as 1478, and its Gothic vaults are adorned with Byzantine-looking frescos.

The great commander and terror of the Turks, Prince Eugene of Savoy, chose Ráckeve as his Hungarian country seat. Begun in 1701, his splendid palace with its formal garden brings a touch of Italian and French sophistication to the rural banks of the Danube.

### THE DANUBE BEND

Budapest and its visitors are fortunate in having so close at hand one of the most spectacular stretches of the Danube. Historic towns and buildings combine with the deep wooded gorge cut by the river to the north of the capital to make this the ideal day excursion, best of all aboard a Danube steamer.

Before it reaches Budapest, the eastward-flowing Danube turns north at the cathedral city of Esztergom. Here it is confronted by the hard rocks of the Pilis and Börzsöny hills, and is forced to carve its way through them in a great bend before splitting into two branches. These make their own way southwards on either side of the 22 mile long (35km) Szentendre 'Island', before joining together again into a single stream just north of the capital.

Road and railway heading north from Budapest pass the remains of **Aquincum**, a reminder that the Danube formed the frontier of civilisation in Roman times. Traces of the forts and milecastles which defended the Empire from the barbarians roaming the wild country beyond can be found all along this stretch of the river.

**Szentendre** itself (easily reached by suburban train), the 'gateway' to the Danube Bend, is one of the most picturesque small towns in Hungary. Its Mediterranean air is perhaps because it was settled originally by southern Slavs (mostly Serbs, but also Dalmatians from the shores of the Adriatic) fleeing from Turkish dominion. In later years the town became something of an artists' colony, its unspoiled beauty and tranquillity attracting people such as the Impressionist artist Károly Ferenczy. A pretty narrow street, Görög utca (Greek Street), rises from the Danube quayside to the small, irregular main square, Fö tér, with its Greek Orthodox cross and fine old houses. On the corner with Görög utca stands one of the town's several fine baroque churches; known as the Greek church, it has a richly decorated interior. Near by are galleries devoted to the work of the Ferenczy family and to the charming work of the sculptor and potter Margit Kovács. The Roman Catholic parish church here is Szentendre's oldest, dating from Romanesque and Gothic times, although rebuilt in baroque style.

Szentendre's other great attraction lies about two miles (3km) away up the valley leading to Visegrád. This is the superb open-air **Szabadtéri Néprajzi Múzeum** (Museum of the Hungarian Village), the best place to get the feel of life as lived in the Hungarian countryside in past centuries. It authentically reproduces farmsteads, stables, churches, mills and even a graveyard.

**Visegrád** is where the narrowest section of the Danube Bend begins. In the Middle Ages the Hungarian kings built the massive **Salamon-torony** (Solomon's Tower) to guard the river bank, as well as another stronghold high above on the ruins of the Roman fort. Their medieval palace was later rebuilt by the great King Matthias, with no expense spared to make a lavish setting for the sophisticated life of his splendid court. Described at the time as a 'paradise on earth', with 350

*Budapest's picturesque Danube*

rooms, hanging gardens and fountains flowing with wine on festive occasions, it fell into ruins under the Turks and remained buried until early this century. Now partly excavated, the remains of the royal palace are revered by Hungarians as a reminder of lost glories.

A scenic road winds high up above the ruins to **Mogyoró-hegy** (Hazelnut Hill). Where once the Hungarian kings hunted, there are now wonderful walks through upland meadows and woodlands, splendid view-points over the gorge and a visitor centre.

These Visegrád Heights (Visegrádi-hegység) are part of the **Pilis Forest Park,** a vast tract of wooded limestone uplands extending far to the southwest. Laced with long-distance footpaths, they reach their highest point at the summit of Pilistetö (2,484 feet/757m).

**Esztergom** is completely dominated by its overwhelming **cathedral,** which, rising from the high rock of the town's Castle Hill, is the biggest church in Hungary. Above the colossal columns of its portico, the huge dome rises to a dizzy height of 352 feet (107m). A catwalk at its base offers staggering views over town, river and surrounding countryside. To the north is the Slovak bank of the Danube, once part of Hungary, but no longer linked directly to Esztergom since the destruction of the road bridge at the end of World War II.

The cathedral was completed in 1856, built over the ruins of its predecessor which had decayed under Turkish rule. It is here that the Roman Catholic primate of Hungary resides, and here that Pope John Paul was received amid much jubilation in 1991. The interior is awe-inspiring rather than beautiful. One relic to have escaped the ravages of time is the Renaissance chapel named after Archbishop Bakócz; others are preserved in the cathedral's Treasury.

From the cathedral precinct, with the reconstructed remains of the medieval royal palace and chapel, there are only slightly less spectacular views than from the dome. The old Víziváros (Watertown), as the lower part of Esztergom is known, spreads out along a side arm of the Danube. The **Keresztény Múzeum** (Christian Museum), housed in the former archbishop's palace, boasts a better collection of medieval art than Budapest.

*Magnificent Esztergom Cathedral*

**Lake Balaton and Area**

Situated some 60 miles (100km) from Budapest, this is Hungary's 'seaside' – since it is actually as inland as anywhere could be, it combines all the best components of water, magnificent scenery and lovely old towns.

As well as the lake itself, the following places are of great interest (some are described in greater detail later): **Tihany** (see page 48) with its high-perched abbey, the old-established spa of **Balatonfüred** (see page 44), and aristocratic **Keszthely** (see page 46).

Vines grow in the flat fields behind the lake's southern shore, and the north bank has some of Hungary's most attractive vineyards. The slopes here are dotted with pretty little buildings for pressing grapes and storing wine. The vines climb almost to the wooded summits of the Balatonifelvidék (uplands). These hills, the southernmost range of the extensive **Bakony Forest,** form an almost continuous backdrop to the lakeside – except in the west, where they give way to the exotic shapes of ancient volcanoes, the **Badacsony Hills** (Badacsony-hegység; see page 43).

Despite the throngs of visitors, nature continues to thrive in and around the lake. Its waters harbour a variety of highly edible fish, of which the *fogas* (pike-perch) is the most famous, while the wetland reserve of **Kis-Balaton** (Little Balaton) is a bird-watchers' paradise, its reed-beds a highly effective system for filtering out impurities brought down by the River Zala. The authorities are very aware of the vulnerability of such a shallow water-body as Balaton to pollution; motor-boating is not allowed on the lake, which of course means there is no water-skiing (except at Balatonfüred, where there is a cable system).

There are many minor treasures to be discovered around the lake, like the strange heart-shaped tombstones in the graveyard at **Balatonudvari**, the old water mill at **Örvényes**, or the well-preserved group of farm buildings at **Szántódpuszta**. Good museums at Siófok (**Beszédes József Hydro-power Museum**) and Keszthely (**Balaton Museum**) fill in some of the fascinating background detail.

Within easy reach is a very different lake at the spa of **Hévíz** (see page 45), whose thermal pool is the largest of its kind in Europe. The historic riches of such cities as **Veszprém** (see page 49) and **Székesfehérvár** (see page 47) are also near by, as are the romantic castles of **Sümeg** (see page 47) and **Nagyvázsony.** Half-way between Balaton and Budapest is **Lake Velence:** much smaller (and, it has to be added, less attractive) than Balaton, it is becoming increasingly popular with those deterred by the steadily rising prices around the shores of its bigger rival. As well as the usual lakeside developments, particularly on the south shore, it is notable for its vast areas of reedbeds, home to countless birds.

◆◆◆
## LAKE BALATON ✓

This beautiful lake is Central Europe's largest, its vast expanse a compensation for Hungarians deprived by history of an outlet to the sea. They throng here to fill the resorts which stud the north shore and extend in an almost continuous line along the beaches of the lake's southern 'coastline'. A multitude of hotels, holiday homes, pensions and flats stand ready to receive them, though everybody's dream is to own a weekend cottage, preferably high up among the vines clinging to the south-facing slopes of the old volcanoes around Badacsony.

The lake is shallow, most of it with an average depth of a mere 10 feet (3m). This makes it safe and enjoyable (if a little muddy) for bathing; the water warms up quickly in summer (reaching the mid-20s°C, mid-70s °F), and the south shore in particular is a paradise for young paddlers. It is also quick to cool in winter, and often freezes over. The lake's mood is normally tranquil, but its lack of depth means that sudden winds can whip up waves of sufficient size to send sailors scurrying for the shore.

Some 50 miles (77km) long, Balaton is divided into two unequal halves by the Tihany peninsula protruding from the north shore. The car ferry landing-point here is only a mile (1.5km) from Szántód on the far side of the straits. This southern shore is generally flat, its main feature being the long string of resorts from Balatonaliga in the east to Balatonberény 44 miles (70km) to the west. The layout of each place tends to follow the same pattern, with the waterside (the 'Strand') backed by parks and sunbathing lawns overlooked by hotels and flats, beyond which is the older part of the settlement, sometimes consisting of an ancient village on the far side of the main road.

At the lake's sole outlet, the River Sió (canalised by the

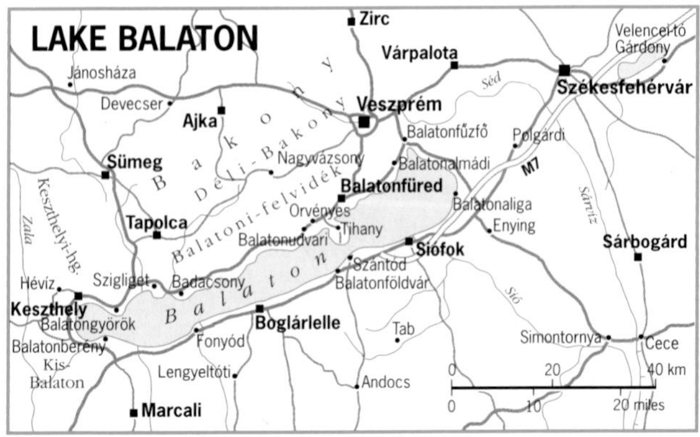

Romans), stands **Siófok**, capital of the south shore, with its 10 miles (15km) of beach. Siófok became fashionable with the well-to-do of Budapest in the 19th century; today the place is unashamedly popular, with high-rise hotels and just a whiff of faded elegance emanating from the few remaining turn-of-the-century villas.

In season, most of the lakeside resorts are linked to one another by ferry services, making it easy to explore. First-time visitors may decide to base themselves somewhere on the north shore, where the hills come close to the lakeside and the shoreline is much more varied. Here the towns and villages have maintained a more distinctive character.

◆
### BADACSONY

This table-topped mountain rises abruptly from the lakeside to a height of 1,437 feet (438m), its basalt cliffs a reminder of its volcanic origin. The shapes of other ancient volcanoes bask peacefully in the countryside around, their lava soils filtering their former force into the vines, which produce some of Hungary's finest wines.

This strange and romantic landscape attracted artists and writers at an early date.

One of the finest perspectives is from the viewpoint near the *csárda* at Balatongyörök to the west.

The more energetic should climb at least one of the hills; Badacsony mountain is topped by a lookout tower, while the remains of **Szigliget Castle** crumble away quietly above Szigliget village. Szigliget was once an island; the village has good examples of houses built in local materials, as well as a basalt-towered church and stately mansions in leafy grounds, one of them the private preserve of the Hungarian Writers' Union.

*Perfect for sailing, the lovely Lake Balaton*

◆◆
## BALATONFÜRED

On any rating of the Balaton resorts, 'Füred' comes out top, with all the usual lakeside facilities in a setting of unusual distinction.

Balatonfüred developed in the 19th century around mineral springs, and consequently has a dignified old core, centred on Gyógy tér (Health Square!). In the middle of the leafy square is the pretty little **Well House**, its temple-like canopy covering the source of the waters. To the north is the charming arcade of the Sanatorium, with cast-iron columns and a pantheon of famous 19th-century visitors. Blaha Lujza utca, lined with old shops, straggles prettily westwards, ending in a squat round church of 1846, while to the south the slope leads down through chestnut trees to the lakeside.

At the eastern end of the tree-lined Promenade is the 'Strand', while at the western end a pier extends into the lake, giving fine views over the great sweep of the bay formed by the Tihany peninsula.

The modern part of town is up the slope to the north, astride the main highway, while the old village which preceded Balatonfüred lies beyond the railway line and still manages to lead a life of its own among the vineyards.

*Hotel with a view at Füred*

### Accommodation

From hotels to trade union hostels, pensions to private houses and 'bungalows', a clear majority of Balatonfüred's buildings are in the business of providing beds for tourists. If you plan to stay here for more than a few days, it would almost certainly be worth while renting an apartment or chalet, either directly or through an agency like IBUSZ.

For a short stay the **Hotel Margherita** offers the standard comforts of a modernish, 3-star, purpose-built establishment. With its own restaurant, it stands among the vineyards a short distance to the west of the centre. Guests have use of the lakeside facilities of a companion hotel, the **Marina.**

Among the profusion of pensions, and conveniently located right in the modern centre at 4 Vörösmarty utca, is the German-orientated **Penzió Korona** (or 'Krone'), with hotel-standard amenities and 'Hungarian home cooking' (tel: 86/43 278).

Just above the lake in the older part of the resort is a big villa in classical style, the **Hotel Blaha Lujza**. All rooms have baths and showers and toilets, and prices are reasonable.

Looking the epitome of the Costa type of high-rise hotel, the **Uni** (on the lake-front just west of the centre) is one of Balatonfüred's many institutional holiday homes, many of which are turning to visitors from abroad to fill their rooms. The institution in this case is the Budapest's Technical University.

**Eating Out**

There are no shortages of places to eat in Balatonfüred, though many of them are crowded in the season. You can choose from hotel restaurants, tourist-orientated *csárdas* and a multitude of private establishments.

In a key position at the Strand end of the Promenade is the **Borcsa.** Its locational advantages have not stopped it trying hard, serving a good range of Hungarian dishes prepared with care. Try the fried *fogas* fillet from the lake or the *veal paprikás.*

Under the same ownership as the Borcsa is the **Halászkert** (Fisherman's Garden), dishing up the specialities suggested by its name. On the main road through town, it is sited right next to Balatonfüred's landmark tourist trap, the restaurant housed in a beached steamboat.

Lying in wait for the tourist trade up in the vineyards near the Margareta Hotel, and offering gypsy music as well as reasonable food, is the **Csárda Hordó** which deserves to be visited at least once.

◆

## HÉVÍZ

The steam rising above the tree-tops at the foot of the Keszthely Hills (Keszthelyi-hegység) marks the site of one of Hungary's great natural curiosities, the thermal lake at Hévíz. Water wells up at a temperature of 35°C to form a deep 10.5 acre (4.7ha) pool, where water lilies bloom. Patients bloom here too: the sulphurous and mildly radioactive water is used successfully to treat patients with muscle and joint problems.

Lake Hévíz is set in attractive parkland. Access to the water is via covered piers adorned with Transylvanian turrets. Health seekers loll in rubber rings on the surface, even in winter, since the water temperature never falls below 25°C.

**Accommodation**

Hévíz consists almost entirely of accommodation. As well as staying in holiday homes, Hungarian visitors rent apartments and private rooms, and anyone contemplating a prolonged stay here should consider doing the same, via an agency like Volántourist, Szabadság út 6 (tel: 82/13 381).

At the top of the range, the modern **Hotel Thermal**, Kossuth L u 9–11 (tel: 82/18 130), offers 4-star comfort plus the full works as far as treatment is concerned (including medical examination, massage, mud-baths, sub-aqua traction), and has its own spectacular indoor pool fed from the spring.

Less expensive but both modern and friendly is the **Panzió Apostól**, Szabadság út 43 (tel: 82/13 151), towards the top of town, and with its own cheerful restaurant.

**Eating Out**
All of the hotels have restaurants, that of the Thermal serving its many guests with great competence. For a change, there is the **Kocsi Csárda**. This is rather unpromisingly sited at the far end of the main car-park at the lower end of Szabadság út; the souvenir stalls *en route* and the gypsy band suggest a tourist trap, but nothing of the kind! The service (in English) is attentive and the food genuine and, for a spa town, inexpensive.

KESZTHELY
Of all the towns around the Balaton, Keszthely alone seems to have some *raison d'être* outside the season. Always a place of importance, it was in the 18th century that it acquired its cultural cachet thanks to the efforts of its local lords, the Festetics family.

The **Festetics Palace** stands at the top (north) end of town, its high and haughty walls forcing the main road round in a loop. It is a massive pile, originally baroque, but much enlarged in the 1880s by Taszilo Festetics. The splendid interior includes a gilt-mirrored ballroom (where summer evening concerts are held) and the famous **Helikon Library.**

The palace is matched by its **park** (partly restored), with its fine trees and fountains, approached through a triumphal gateway. In the face of all this magnificence, the town seems somewhat faded. Its cultural heyday was under Festetics rule in the 19th century, when learned societies and theatrical activities flourished. A new lease of life came with the growing fashion for lakeside holidays at the end of the century. All this, and much more besides, is nicely evoked in the excellent exhibition 'Balaton and Man', pride of the good **Local Museum**.

**Accommodation**
A number of hotels guard the shore near the pier and ferry landing, ranging from the large, modern, 3-star **Helikon**, Balaton-part 5 (tel: 82/18 944), which makes much of its wide range of sporting facilities, to the more modest 2-star **Phoenix**, Balaton-part 3 (tel: 82/12 630). There is also private accommodation in modern chalet-type houses – ask at the station.

**Eating Out**
As you might expect, there is a **Halászcsárda** (fish restaurant) by the lake, while inland, installed in a typical Hungarian single-storey house in a quiet part of town (Vörösmarty u 1a), the **Park Vendéglö** serves honest, heavy food.

SÜMEG
The dreamy little town of Sümeg is dominated by the very substantial remains of its castle, which has featured in most of the violent disturbances that litter Hungarian history, from troubles with the Turks to the Rákóczi Rebellion. The trek to the top is worth it for the view alone.

The castle is approached via Szent István tér; as well as a number of pretty, old houses and a fine baroque church, the square has the palace built by Bishop Biró of Veszprém around 1750.

**Light in the Church**
Tucked into a delightful little square, the mid-18th-century **Parish Church** has a plain exterior belying the glories within. A 10 forint coin will light up a series of theatrically animated scenes, based on the life of Christ, painted with splendid verve by the Austrian Franz Anton Maulbertsch. Here, this great church painter was working on the orders of Bishop Biró, who, perhaps not surprisingly, had himself immortalised among the heavenly hosts (above the organ).

◆◆
## SZÉKESFEHÉRVÁR

Székesfehérvár (Sake-esh-fur-hair-var) occupies a special place in Hungarian hearts; the place where, for hundreds of years, the country's kings were crowned and many of them buried. Occupation by the Turks put paid to this tradition, and when they finally withdrew, Székesfehérvár had to be rebuilt. The fine new baroque churches, public buildings and town houses were fitted into the medieval pattern of crooked streets and odd-shaped squares. The result is a treat for the visitor's eye.
The best (and chronologically correct) place to start is the **Romkert,** the Garden of Ruins, where the remains of King Stephen's Coronation Church are best viewed from the elevated public pavement. Szabadság (Freedom) tér beyond has an array of imposing civic buildings, easily dominated by the swaggering **Bishop's Palace.** This was built at the end of the 18th century by Bishop János Milassin, who did not shrink from completing the work of the Turks by demolishing what was left of the Coronation Church, and using the stones to construct his monumental residence. At the centre of the square stands a great stone orb, the first of many memorials (of variable aesthetic quality) put up all around the town as part of the celebrations commemorating the 900th anniversary of King Stephen's death.
To the south, cobbled streets and steps rise to the baroque **cathedral,** built on the spot where Prince Géza erected his castle in 970. Standing almost

*The faded beauty of Székesfehérvár*

apologetically at the side of the cathedral is the little **St Anne's Chapel**, the town's only Gothic building to remain intact. It is worth while going a little further downhill towards the triangular István tér, if only to take in two Art Nouveau interruptions to the ancient townscape; a galleried house with delicate floral ornamentation, and Székesfehérvár's oriental-looking spa building.
The town's main street, Március 15 utca, curves northwards from Szabadság tér, slowly straightening itself out, and culminating in the extremely self-important square. This is dominated by the town's theatre (named after the poet Vörösmarty) and the grand hotel (named after the Hungarian king).

*Figure in Tihany's Abbey Church*

In the eastern part of the town, in an incongruous setting of suburban houses, is **Bory's Castle**. This utterly individual amalgam of towers and turrets, cupolas and courtyards, gardens and statuary, defying all attempts at categorisation, was the result of the lifelong labours of the sculptor Jenö Bory.

### Accommodation

The **Alba Regia**, Rákóczi u 1 (tel: 22/13 484), 3-star, is modern, offering reasonable comforts in an excellent position on the edge of the old town centre (by the Garden of Ruins). Complete with café, restaurant and night club, it is one of Székesfehérvár's social centres too.
**Hotel Magyar Király** (Hungarian King), Március 15, u 10 (tel: 22/11 262), 2-star, is half the size of the Alba Regia but is housed in a dignified classical building dating from the mid-19th century. Restaurant and brasserie.
**Panzió Dominó,** Fiskális u (tel: 22/25 279) is a small family-run pension and pleasant restaurant on the outskirts of town, near the bypass and Bory's Castle.

### Eating Out

Available in all the above, plus the **Ösfehérvár Étterem** in Szabadság tér.

## TIHANY

Its natural beauties, historic associations and splendid abbey church high above Lake Balaton make the Tihany peninsula a popular destination for Hungarians and their visitors.

The long tongue of land, once almost separated from the mainland by marshes, protrudes three miles (5km) into the lake, dividing it into two distinct parts.

The whole of the peninsula is a nature reserve, worth exploring on foot to see its two little lakes and the strange cones formed by the hundred or so geysers which burst forth half a million years ago. The view of the two halves of the lake from the Csúcs hilltop is one of Balaton's best.

However, most of the multitudes who flock to Tihany do not come with hiking in mind. This is a place thoroughly given over to tourism; the Strand down by the ferry landing on Tihany's southern tip has its adherents, but the key attraction is the lovely late baroque **Abbey Church** rising invitingly above Tihany village. Modern pilgrims tread the steps and ramps from the car-park to the cobbled square in front of the church, and peer briefly round its interior before strolling along the spectacular hill-top promenade beyond.

The inside of the church rates more than a casual glance. Contrasting with the sophistication of the usual array of fine baroque altarpieces is the raw stonework of an 11th-century crypt, a reminder of the remote world of the early Magyars. Here is the tombstone of Andrew I, the only grave of an Arpad king to have remained in its original location. Joined to the church, the main monastery building is now a museum, while the stables and other outbuildings have been turned into a courtyard café – expensive, but with stunning views over the lake.

Behind its veil of multilingual tourist signboards, Tihany has managed to keep something of its village character. Some of its old houses, built by peasants and fisherfolk out of basalt tufa, have been lovingly restored; the **Fishermen's Guild Museum** is worth seeing too.

### Accommodation

Tihany has accommodation ranging from the luxury of the **Tihany Club**, Rév u 3 (tel: 86/48 088) in its exclusive position at the ferry landing, or the **Kolostor,** Kossuth u 14 (tel: 86/48 408) in the upper village, to private rooms. But it is generally recognised as one of the most expensive places in Hungary. It is the ideal destination for a day out, from Balatonfüred for example, which has more facilities.

### Eating Out

The **Rege Café** housed in some of the abbey's outbuildings (see above) profits from its position as a kind of compulsory stop on the tourist trail.

The **Kolostor** (see above) has a choice of restaurant or brasserie.

## VESZPRÉM

This bustling county and university town owes its fame to its associations with Hungary's royal past, and its distinction to the historic buildings crowning the rocky promontory of **Castle Hill** which rises from the modern town centre.

A tradition grew up in the Middle Ages that the bishop of Veszprém would have the privilege of crowning the queens of Hungary. The very first of the country's queens, **Gisela of Bavaria**, stands as a more than life-size stone sculpture next to her husband, **King Stephen**. To reach her, start walking (cars not allowed) from Óváros tér, an irregularly shaped square with some Art Nouveau buildings. The entrance to Castle Hill is marked by the 1930s neo-Romanesque **Heroes' Gate** (with a small museum) and the 19th-century **Tüztorony** (Firetower). Beyond, the charming cobbled street has some fine noblemen's town houses as well as a former college and its church, all dating from the 18th and early 19th century, since Veszprém had to be rebuilt from scratch after the expulsion of the Turks. The street widens out to become a square, the core of Castle Hill, where queen and bishop resided in some state. The **Bishop's Palace,** all in white, is particularly grand, the Franciscans' church and the cathedral rather less so.

*Keszthely Palace*

Just to the north of the cathedral the ruins of a 12th-century chapel are preserved under glass, while off the square is a masterpiece of early Gothic building, the chapel known as the **Gizella-kápolna.**

To the south of the busy shopping precincts of the town centre is an attractively landscaped area, embedded in which is a stunning Art Nouveau structure. Named after the poet Petöfi and lavishly restored, this houses the town's theatre. A little further out is the **Bakony Museum,** and next to it a reconstructed rural house, no peasant's hut, but the authentically furnished dwelling of a member of the minor gentry.

**Accommodation**

Most visitors to Veszprém will have made it their destination for a day trip from Balaton, but it is possible to stay here. The **Veszprém Hotel**, Budapest u 6 (tel: 80/24 876), 2-star, is modern and central; the **Erdei** (Forest) **Motel**, Kittenberger K u 14 (tel: 80/26 751) less so.

**Eating Out**

The **Veszprém Hotel** has a conventional hotel restaurant, or you could try the **Pusztai Restaurant** in Buhim utca.

## WESTERN HUNGARY

Sharing borders with Slovakia, Austria, Slovenia and Croatia, western Hungary is a region of great landscape variety with more than its fair share of the country's historic places.
The traveller hurrying between Vienna and Budapest or Balaton may only remember the impression of monotony conveyed by the Kisalföld (the Little Plain), its rich farmlands stretching featurelessly south of the Danube. But contrasting with this steppe-like lowland are the landscapes all around its edge; these range from the wetlands of the many-channelled Danube and Lake Fertö, to the wooded uplands of the Bakony Forest dividing the region from Lake Balaton and the 'Hungarian Alps' of the border country fringing Austria. Many of the towns are built on Roman foundations. The medieval Magyars built castles aplenty in their western frontier region, together with prosperous trading towns and the churches and monasteries of the Christian religion adopted by their rulers. Less devastated by the Mongol invasion of 1242, this part of the country also remained largely free from the long Turkish occupation, giving its towns a continuity of building rare elsewhere in Hungary.
This is seen above all in Sopron, one of Europe's great historic cities, but there are fascinating smaller places too, like exquisite Köszeg. The area's prosperity and its proximity to Vienna and the imperial court meant that much building and rebuilding took place in baroque times – in Györ for example, the capital of the Little Plain, while the most sumptuous of all Hungary's palaces was erected for Prince Esterházy at Fertöd.

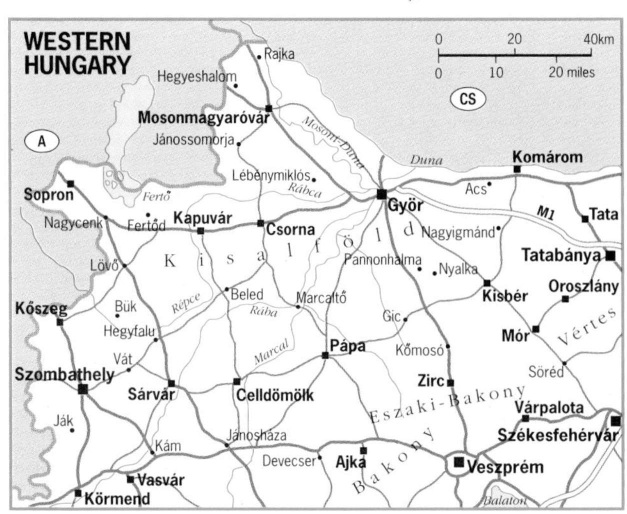

◆◆◆
## FERTÖD

'I discovered a Versailles' exclaimed the French ambassador after visiting the stupendous rococo palace built here by Prince Miklós Esterházy ('The Magnificent') in the 1760s. The Esterházy family had benefited from their loyalty to the Habsburgs to accumulate vast landed estates. Their fabulous wealth was the foundation on which Prince Miklós built the extravagant lifestyle for which Fertöd – originally named Esterháza – was the splendid setting.

Like the palace of Versailles, Fertöd was not just a residence, but a complex of buildings and landscapes designed to contain the varied activities of a princely court and its many guests. The structures included an Opera Hall, Music House, Puppet Theatre, Chinese Banqueting Hall, and a Hermitage, while exotic plants and animals flourished in enclosed gardens and guests could hunt their quarry through the well-stocked game park. The great composer Josef Haydn was Prince Miklós' faithful director of music for many years, both here and at the other Esterházy palace at Eisenstadt/Kismarton (now just

*The effortless elegance of Esterházy Palace*

across the border in Austria). After Miklós' death in 1790, the palace's great days were over: buildings gradually decayed and grounds ran wild, and the place suffered badly in World War II. Since then, careful restoration work has done much to bring back former glories.

Outside the gates of the main entrance are the buildings (now a café) which once housed the grenadiers of the prince's bodyguard. Haydn's quarters were in the baroque Music House.

◆◆

**GYÖR**

Trapped in the traffic grinding along highway 1 through the undistinguished southern outskirts of Györ, you could be forgiven for hurrying eastwards to Budapest or west to Vienna. But this cathedral city at the junction of the southern branch of the Danube with the Rábca and Rába rivers deserves much more than a backward glance. Left in ruins after only a brief Turkish occupation (1594–8), it was rebuilt in best baroque style. The capital of the Kisalföld, it is a lively place too, especially when the Saturday market fills Duna-kapu tér.

Old Györ has two centres. One, a web of narrow streets, steps and alleyways converging on the cathedral, occupies the rising ground known as the **Káptalan-domb,** while to the east is **Széchenyi Square,** focus of a chequerboard of shopping streets.

The **cathedral** rises grandly over its cobbled square. On 11th-century foundations, it bears traces of most building periods, though it is essentially a baroque structure with an early 19th-century west front. Its great treasure is a masterpiece of the medieval goldsmith's art, the **reliquary bust** of St Ladislas (Szent Laszló), the second Hungarian king (after Stephen) to be made a saint. At the foot of the slope down from the cathedral, the fortifications which failed to keep the Turks out can be explored, from no 5 Köztársaság tér (Republic Square), which also houses stonework finds. This square is dominated by the **Church of the Carmelites**. In contrast to the cathedral, this fine baroque edifice took only a short time to complete (1721–5), and consequently has a beautifully harmonious appearance.

The busy streets leading eastwards will bring you to Széchenyi tér; on the way there is much to admire, like the fine baroque residences on the east side of Köztársaság tér, or the Napoleon House at no 4 Alkotmány utca (with a picture gallery). With its tall column dedicated to the Virgin Mary, Széchenyi tér is dominated by the early baroque **Church of St Ignatius** attached to its former Jesuit monastery. Opposite is the **János Xantus Museum**, housed in the Györ *pied-à-terre* of the abbot of Pannonhalma, which presents the archaeology and history of the city and its surroundings in exemplary fashion.

A stroll in any direction from the square will reveal something of interest. Just to the east, next to the pretty Church of St Anne, are the two tiny courtyards of the 17th-century Hungarian hospital, with a tasteful modern bird fountain. Two blocks to the south stands Györ's massive modern **Kisfaludy Theatre,** named after the dramatist Károly Kisfaludy, born here in 1788; the bold ceramic decoration is by the Pécs pioneer of Op Art, Victor Vasarely. In the opposite direction, towards the Danube quayside, is a gallery devoted to the work of another famous native of Györ, the sculptress/ ceramicist Margit Kovács (in the Kreszta House, Rózsa Ferenc u 1); nearby, the splendid baroque sculpture of the Ark of the Covenant was designed by the Viennese architect Joseph Emanuel Fischer von Erlach.

*The timeless atmosphere of Köszeg*

**Accommodation**

**Rába Hotel**, Árpád u 34 (tel: 96/15 533), 3-star, large modern high-rise hotel in the city centre just off highway 1. **Klastrom Hotel**, Zechmeister u 1 (tel: 96/15 611), 3-star, in a prime position on the banks of the Rába, near Köztársaság tér. Restaurant, bar, brasserie.

Two good central *panziós*: **Ringa**, Czuczor Gergely u 12–14 (tel: 96/10 262), situated in an impeccably converted butcher's shop with a restaurant and Tokay wine-cellar. **Teatrum Panzió** with restaurant, Schweidel út 7 (tel: 96/10 640), a large, 'luxury' pension, alongside the theatre.

**Eating Out**

Very convenient for sightseers is the **Várkapu** at the side of the ramp leading up to the cathedral. Moderate prices. Cheaper and altogether more 'local' is the **Sárkánylyuk** (Dragon's Cave) in Kazinczy út. Expert service in a small space.

◆◆

## KÖSZEG

At the foot of the wooded hills marking the border with Austria, this idyllic little town is one of the most picturesque in Hungary. Köszeg's medieval walls and **castle** are reminders that the town stood guard over Hungary's vulnerable western frontier; in 1532 a handful of defenders under the leadership of the Croat commander Niklas Jurisich (Miklós Jurisics in Hungarian) brought the Turkish advance on Vienna to a full stop. Jurisics received the castle as a reward; approached via a pleasingly irregular courtyard, it now houses the museum.

Explore the intimate old streets and absorb details like statues in niches, venerable doorways or the painted medallions of the **Town Hall**. This stands in the town's delightful central square, **Jurisics tér**, with its little baroque column dedicated to the Virgin Mary. To the north are the twin churches of St James and St Imre, to the south, the 'Heroes' Gate'. But it is the more modest buildings around the edge of the square which contribute most to the timeless atmosphere; among them is (inevitably!) an old **apothecary**, a specially fine example dating from the early 1700s.

### Accommodation

**Strucc**, Várkör 124 (tel: 94/60 323),1-star, in a fine building close to the medieval centre. Not all rooms have their own bath, but all are very competitively priced. This is reputedly the oldest hotel in Hungary. Café with dartboard.

### Eating Out

**Bécsi kapu** (Vienna Gate) brasserie, Rajnis u 5. A medieval atmosphere re-created in the vaults of one of the town's ancient houses. Good fare and wines at reasonable prices.

## PANNONHALMA

This is Hungary's greatest monastic foundation, founded on its sacred hilltop site a thousand years ago, and dominating the quiet countryside for miles around. In 996 Prince Géza brought in Benedictine monks from the West, part of the Hungarian monarchy's planned conversion of the country to Christianity. The project succeeded, Pannonhalma in particular being responsible for the founding of many daughter abbeys, like Tihany on Lake Balaton in 1055.

The monastery burnt down at the time of the Turkish troubles, and was closed altogether in 1786–1802 when the Benedictine Order was dissolved. It survived the Communist regime intact, together with its private boarding school – a rare achievement.

The buildings mostly date from the early 19th century; the great tower, 180 feet (55m) high, was completed in 1830. Inside, the feeling of medieval piety is still conveyed by the much restored abbey church, crypt, and cloisters. The superb 300,000-volume library is far and away the largest of its kind in the country. Among Pannonhalma's priceless treasures is the foundation deed of Tihany Abbey – the very first document to contain words written in Hungarian as well as the usual Latin.

### Accommodation

Only a short distance south of Györ and the Vienna–Budapest highway, Pannonhalma is a possible place to break your journey, at the modern (but traditionally styled) and moderately priced 3-star **Pax Hotel** (tel: 96/70-006), with restaurant, bar, sauna. English spoken.

## SOPRON

At the centre of a strange bulge in the Austro-Hungarian border and at the foot of the Lövér Hills stands Sopron, the country's most self-consciously historic city. With more listed buildings and monuments to its name than anywhere else in Hungary outside the capital, Sopron's wonderfully complete state of preservation is due to its position in the extreme west of the country, out of reach of both Mongol and Turk. Rebuilding here was carried out, not in response to wholesale destruction (though the city did suffer in the final weeks of World War II), but through a desire for embellishment and improvement. Many of the town's medieval buildings rest on Roman foundations, and conceal their antiquity behind a baroque or Renaissance façade.

The old town is horseshoe-shaped, ringed by the substantial remains of its medieval defensive walls (built on the earlier foundations of a Roman wall), around which runs the boulevard-like Várkerület, busy with coach parties of Viennese who have nipped across the border on half-day shopping trips. Behind the Elö kapu (Outer Gate) looms the city's emblem, the **Firetower**. Originally used as a look-out tower to warn of fire, it is well worth the climb for the reward of the best view over Sopron's rooftops. Some 200 feet (60m) high, it seems to encapsulate the city's architectural history, rising from (square) Roman foundations through a (cylindrical) medieval lower section to a Renaissance gallery and baroque onion dome and belfry.

Overlooked by the Firetower is the ancient core of Sopron, **Fö tér** (Main Square), at its centre a particularly splendid Plague Column, along its north side a trio of proud patrician houses. The corner building is known as the **Storno House**, dating originally from the 15th century but with many later features including a fine Renaissance courtyard; inside are items of furniture and other household objects assembled by the Storno family, as well as a municipal museum. Number 7,

*Sopron's distinctive Firetower*

**Exploring old Sopron**

All three streets running south from Fö tér are worth wandering through at a leisurely pace. No false notes disturb the architectural harmony and there are plenty of highlights too, like the Esterházys' town *pied-à-terre* at no 2 Templom utca, the two synagogues in Új utca, another trio of fine residences at nos 12–16 Szent György utca, and the splendid stuccoed interior of St George's Church opposite. Eventually you will find yourself in the tiny Orsolya tér with its central fountain, or you may choose to leave the old centre altogether via the grand 19th-century Széchenyi tér to the south.

also with a courtyard, is called the **Lackner House** after a 17th-century mayor and no 8, the **Fabricius House**, hiding its medieval origins behind a baroque façade, is also a museum, with interesting archaeological finds and much else besides.

On the far side of the square is the city's principal place of worship, the Gothic **Church of St Mary**, popularly known as the 'Goat Church' (Kecske-templom), since its construction is supposed to have been financed by a hoard of treasure unearthed here by a humble goatherd. Behind it is the **Chapter House**, once part of a Franciscan monastery; beneath its vaults are relief sculptures depicting the Deadly Sins.

*The view from Sopron's Firetower is well worth the climb*

## Excursion from Sopron

### NAGYCENK

Some 8 miles (13km) from Sopron, this dignified mansion with its formal garden and British park was the home of 'the greatest Hungarian', Count István Széchenyi (1791–1860), the far-sighted aristocrat who, by urging and by example, dragged a backward nation into the modern age. Taking Britain, then the 'workshop of the world' as his model, he promoted projects like the Chain Bridge in Budapest, steam navigation on the Danube and Lake Balaton, and the building of a network of railways.

His progressive views found expression here in his own home: Nagycenk was the first place in Hungary to be lit by gas and to have flush toilets!

Badly damaged in World War I, and since then carefully restored, the family mansion now houses a hotel as well as Széchenyi's **Memorial Museum**. At the end of the lime-tree avenue is the **Railway Museum**, complete with veteran locomotives, rolling stock and an antique station building.

**Accommodation**

The old area just north of the centre of Sopron has several possibilities. These include the **Hotel Sopron**, Fövenyverem u 7 (tel: 99/14 254),3-star, a large and lavish modern hotel, with restaurant, brasserie, night-club, fitness room etc. Less expensive than you might think, and with a resident dentist (it is cheaper for Austrians to have their teeth seen to here than at home).

**The Jégverem Fogadó**, Jégverem u 1 (tel: 99/12 004) is a snappy modern building intriguingly constructed around the old municipal ice-cellar. Graded as a top-category *panzio*, it has standards and prices to match.

The **Panzio Bástya**, Patak u 40, is housed in a somewhat forbidding building just off the Bécsi u. Good value.

Near by, at **Bécsi út 38** (tel: 99/34 028), are very pleasant rooms (bathrooms on corridor) in a large private house.

Out of town, you can stay *chez* Széchenyi at the **Kastély Hotel**, Nagycenk, Kiscenki út 3 (tel: 97/41 586), 3-star.

The **Red Mansion** on the great count's estate has been converted into a small and elegant hotel, with restaurant and many other facilities.

**Eating Out**

Both the **Sopron** and the **Jégverem** have restaurants, the latter with the tables neatly arranged around the opening to the ice-cellar. In between are two characterful places to eat, the **Halászcsárda,** its fish specialities indicated by its sign, and the **Bécsi Kapu,** a wine restaurant approached down an atmospherically cobbled and vaulted passageway.

*End of excursion*

◆

SZOMBATHELY

The capital of Vas county, Szombathely ('som bat hay') has long been an important centre of administration, commerce and culture. It is worth visiting for its large historic town centre which provides plenty of interest for a good half day's urban stroll.

The Roman remains here are some of the most important north of the Alps. They are in two separate clusters. Behind the cathedral is the **Romkert** (Garden of Ruins), with a basalt-block paved stretch of a Roman road as well as a fine mosaic floor which belonged to the early Christian basilica erected here in the 4th century. The second cluster of buildings was devoted to the exotic cult of the Egyptian goddess Isis and resulted in the **Iseum**, to the southeast.

The centre of modern Szombathely is the large triangular Köztársaság tér, whose market stalls and tramcars have given way to extravagant efforts at landscaping. To the west of the square and the Garden of Ruins is the ecclesiastical quarter, with its overbearing late baroque/early classical **cathedral** and bishop's palace. Around the Iseum to the south is another focus of interest. The oriental-looking synagogue is now the Bartók Concert Hall. The long, low and mostly concrete art gallery dominating the grounds of the Iseum is a bit too big for its contents, though the passionately-felt Socialism of the revolutionary artists Gyula Derkovits (1894–1934) and István Dési Huber (1895–1944) still makes itself felt.

**A Collection of Curiosities**
The most original 'sight' in Szombathely is the **Smidt Museum**. A modest town residence near the cathedral, it houses the fruits of surgeon Lajos Smidt's life-long squirrel-like collecting activity. Its rooms are filled with arms and uniforms, coins and pots, clocks, medical memorabilia – and much else besides.

### Accommodation

**Savaria**, Mártírok tere 4 (tel: 94/11 440), 2-star, is a huge Art Nouveau pile in the town centre with reasonably priced rooms and a high-ceilinged restaurant. Two pensions: the dental practice (!) in Sebes György utca (central) has a number of rooms with bath at very reasonable prices (tel: 94/18 555), while the **Nardai Kastély Fogadó** (tel: 98/12 481) is three miles (5km) outside town on the way to the village of Narda.

### Eating Out

There is excellent hearty eating at the comfortable and unpretentious **Gyöngyös Étterem**, Savaria u 8. Try to arrange to be here after their butcher has just slaughtered his best pigs and turned them into a delicious variety of sausages.

*Trombitas Restaurant: Hungarians will use any excuse to enjoy good food and wine with family and friends*

## SOUTHERN HUNGARY

South from Budapest the Danube's mood changes. There is little of the drama of the Danube Bend or the excitement of the quaysides and bridges of the capital. Instead, the great river flows quietly between the banks protecting the mostly flat countryside from the river's springtime floodwaters.
Away from the river, to the west, is an unspectacular but attractive countryside of low hills divided by tranquil river valleys. After the Turks had finally been driven out of Hungary, much of this area was repopulated by settlers who sailed down the Danube from Germany. Collectively known as 'Swabians', though only a minority of them came from that part of southern Germany, they gave their new homeland the ironic-sounding name of 'Swabian Turkey'. Though many of their descendants left Hungary after World War II, others remain in villages of distinctly German character. Hungary's southernmost county, Baranya, is one of the country's most individual regions. Protected from northern blasts by the imposing Mecsek uplands – highest point Zengö, 2,238 feet (682m) – this is where Central Europe begins to take on Mediterranean colouring. The county capital, Pécs, has an enviable situation at the foot of the lower, vine-clad slopes of the Mecsek. It is one of Hungary's most fascinating cities, a modern, lively place but with many layers of the past too, from Roman remains to the former mosque dominating the city's main square. Further south still towards the River Dráva, marking the border with Croatia, a final range of Hungarian hills, the Villányi-hegység, produces some of the country's famous wines, as well as sheltering the spa of Harkány and the castle town of Siklós.

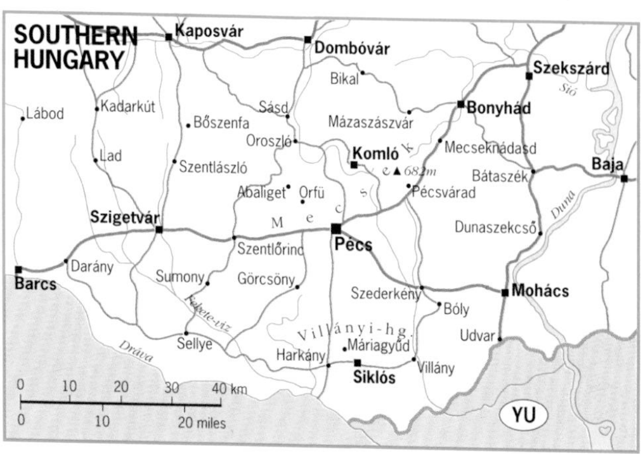

## PÉCS ✓

There are many reasons for visiting this ancient and flourishing city: its monuments spanning the centuries, its exceptional museums and galleries, its huge Sunday market, its position as a centre for excursions into the Mecsek and Villány Hills – perhaps most of all for its undeniable air of a provincial capital, a place whose urban pleasures compete with those of the metropolis without the attendant stress and strain.

*The attractive town of Pécs, nestled in the Mecsek and Villány Hills*

The Romans called Pécs, *Sopianae* and made it the centre of the province of southern Pannonia. By the Middle Ages it had been renamed *Quinque Ecclesiae* (Five Churches). The town was the site of Hungary's first university, opened in 1367 in the reign of Louis of Anjou. Despite occupation by the Turks from 1543 it continued to prosper – though its Habsburg 'liberators' in 1686 found most of the city in ruins. Rebuilding was slow, but in the later19th century coal helped make the place wealthy again, and until recently the nearby uranium mines supplied much of the Soviet need for this strategic mineral.

**Free for a week**
A bizarre interlude in Pécs' history occurred in 1919–21, when it was occupied by Yugoslav troops and enjoyed a very brief period of independence (one week!) from Admiral Horthy's Hungary as the capital of the 'Baranya Republic'.

Explorations of Pécs tend to begin and end in Széchenyi tér, whose gentle slope is a last reminder of the Mecsek hills to the north. Sitting comfortably towards the top of the square is Hungary's most important Turkish building, the domed **Mosque of Gazi Kassim Pasha**, a substantial stone edifice of 1580, whose architect had no compunction in re-using the walls of the medieval Christian church which once stood on the site. Re-Christianised and now serving as the city centre parish church, this is one of the emblems of Pécs.

A number of self-consciously important buildings line the square and confirm its role as the epicentre of the city's life. Among them is the **Hotel Nádor** (currently undergoing reconstruction), whose café once buzzed to the conversation of the turn-of-the-century intellectual élite.

The streets radiating from the square offer many pleasant surprises, from pretty baroque façades to coy coffee-houses, and deserve careful exploration. As in so many Hungarian towns, the Art Nouveau period left its highly distinctive mark on the townscape. The post office in Jókai utca is a confident example of the genre, while the synagogue in Kossuth tér, though earlier in date (1869) is equally elaborate.

Starting from the northwest corner of the Széchenyi tér, Janus Pannonius utca leads towards the green islands of St István tér and Dóm tér, above which rise the four towers of the **cathedral**. This is one of the great churches of Hungary, begun in the 11th century, a mosque too in its time, and restored somewhat grandiloquently in the 19th century in an attempt to recover its original appearance. The oldest part still intact is the five-aisled crypt. The spacious interior forms a fine setting for concerts.

Beneath the square there are fascinating traces of the early days of Christianity (unique in Hungary), and a Roman mausoleum and burial chamber, both with wall paintings and both beautifully preserved and presented.

Beyond the strange metal sculpture of Liszt leaning from the balcony of the baroque bishop's palace on the west side of the cathedral square stands a round tower complete with drawbridge, a relic of the city defences whose remaining walls run alongside the ring road to the north.

Beyond the city walls in Rákóczi ut is the **Mosque of Jakovali Hassan Pasha**, still, unusually, with its minaret intact.

Good views over the city can be enjoyed from the Tettye plateau (with its dervish

monastery) to the northeast of the city wall, and from the Calvary chapel and stations of the cross just above the cathedral.

Pécs has all the cultural buzz to be expected in a provincial capital, not least because of its four institutions of higher education (two universities and two colleges). The prestige of the city's drama, opera, music, ballet and marionette companies is expressed in the painstakingly restored 19th-century façade of the **National Theatre** in Kossuth Lajos utca.

Firmly rooted in its past, Pécs is by no means backward looking. Alternatives to the facelessness of much recent building are proposed in light-hearted post modern structures like the **Hotel Fönix** (no 2 Hunyadi utca) or the **Solar House** of 1986, while contemporary artistic efforts can be seen in the numerous galleries.

*The bustling colourful Sunday market draws the crowds*

### Accommodation

**Palatinus Hotel**, Kossuth L u 5 (tel: 72/33 022),3-star. Opposite the National Theatre, this is a superbly restored Art Nouveau monument, with one of the best interiors of its kind in Hungary. The ballroom is particularly sumptuous. Restaurant, café, brasserie.

**Nádor**, Széchenyi tér 15 (tel: 72/11 477), 2-star. Originally built in the mid-19th century, this traditional rendezvous of Pécs' élite in the heart of town is currently undergoing restoration. Restaurant, café, brasserie, patisserie.

**Fönix Hotel**, Hunyadi u 2 (tel: 72/13 322), small, highly individual building in innovative style (see above), close to the mosque. Its pizzeria always seems to be crowded with the city's gilded youth.

### Eating Out

There is no shortage of places to eat and drink in this southern city. The restaurant of the **Palatinus Hotel** offers good food in its turn-of-the-century ambience, while on the same side of Kossuth u, reached through an arched and cobbled passageway, is the snug **Dóm brasserie**, serving its own wine from the Villány Hills as well as Hamburg beer.

Particularly popular with young people are the pizzeria of the **Fönix**, and the **Barbakan**. The latter forms part of the city wall in Landler u and has a wine bar next door, too.

Summer evenings can be pleasantly spent in a number of places among the vineyards above the city – try **Fenyves** (also a hotel), Szölö u 64.

### Excursions from Pécs

All the following places make good day or half-day excursions from Pécs.

◆

### MECSEK HILLS

A scenic road winds its way up through magnificent lime and oak woods of this limestone massif, giving ever more extensive views over Pécs and the country beyond. A first stopping point could be the massive **Liberation Monument** commemorating the arrival of the Red Army in late 1944, but the truly spectacular panorama is the one from the top of the TV tower rising dizzily from the summit. Pécs can be seen sitting snugly in the sun, facing southwards, protected by the mountain from the north, garlanded with the green of its garden allotments and weekend cottages.

The Mecsek woodlands are threaded with hiking trails. On the northern slopes of the upland are a number of local resorts based on a chain of artificial lakes, much used by swimmers and other watersports enthusiasts. There is a Mill Museum in the village of **Orfü**, and stalactite caves at **Abaliget**.

The region's mixed ethnic heritage can be traced towards the eastern end of the range, where a number of villages bear an unmistakably Germanic stamp. Just off the main Budapest–Pécs highway is the fascinating village of **Mecseknádasd**, its 18th-century colonists' farmsteads evenly spaced along the street, at one end of which there is a village museum telling something of the history of the local 'Swabians'.

◆

### MOHÁCS

The town lies to the east of Pécs. Mohács is a doom-laden name for Hungarians. A spacious memorial park, four miles (7km) south of the town commemorates the country's terrible defeat here at the hands of the Turks in 1526, when the troops of Suleiman the Magnificent crushed the army of King Louis II. Ten days after the Hungarian king had died ignominiously in a ditch, his adversary was making himself at home in the castle at Buda. The imaginative, somewhat eerie timber totems of the memorial, a far cry from conventional monuments of this kind, evoke something of the horrors of the battlefield. A museum on the Danube side of the town vividly recalls the disaster.

Mohács is perhaps best known for its famous carnival. On 1 March, grotesquely-masked revellers parade through the streets in a festival of Serbian origin designed to put winter to flight and adapted to celebrate the eventual expulsion of the Turks.

◆

## SIKLÓS

This pleasant town, some 19 miles (30km) south of Pécs is dominated by its **castle**, begun in the 13th century. It is unusually complete for Hungary, with barbicans, bastions, dungeons filled with instruments of torture, and a Gothic chapel with wall-paintings. It is also a hotel, restaurant and wine-cellar!

Just northwest of the town on the road from Pécs is the village of **Máriagyüd**, with a prominent twin-towered pilgrimage church dating from the early 18th century. Pilgrims flock here in search of healing, their diverse ethnic origin attested to by the inscriptions in German and Croatian as well as Hungarian. A wine-cellar by the church steps supplies other comforts.

Above the road from Siklós to Villány is an old marble quarry, since 1968 a sculpture park. Every year sculptors from all over the world take part in a symposium here; the marble is supplied free, but the sculpture stays behind! The result is a fascinatingly variegated collection of individual, sometimes eccentric pieces, well worth pausing for.

*Wine tasting at Villány*

◆

## VILLÁNY

Some of Hungary's most delicious red wine comes from the south-facing slopes of this low range of hills. What appear to be unusually modest village houses strung out along the main road running along the foot of the hills are in fact wine-cellars, dug into the hillside and reeking of the vintage slowly maturing in the rows of barrels. Vines have been grown here since Roman times. The activities and traditions of more recent wine-growers (many of German origin – Villány is Wieland in German) are explained in the **wine museum**.

## NORTHERN HUNGARY

Northeastwards from Budapest, a broad band of forested uplands divides Hungary's Great Plain from Czechoslovakia. Though the much higher Tatras and Fatras on the far side of the border continue to attract many Hungarians (Slovakia – or Upper Hungary as it was then known – was the playground for rich Budapesters in the days before World War I), these modest mountains – highest point Kékesteto, 3,330 feet (1,015m) – are much appreciated for their (fairly sparse) winter sports facilities as well as their fresh air in the summer.

Castles, intact or in ruins, abound in this border region, whose relative remoteness has preserved many traces of the traditional architecture and way of life of different ethnic groups.

The mountains divide into a series of ranges, each with its own distinctive character. The volcanic Börzsöny hills running northwards from the Danube Bend offer hikers much the same pleasures as the Pilis Forest Park to the south, though they attract far fewer visitors. They are separated from the much more popular Mátra Mountains by the lower Cserehát range, much of whose woodland has disappeared but which is home to the colourful and mysterious Palóc ethnic group (see page 71). Using the raw materials of the mountains (wood for charcoal, metal ores), industry came early to these parts. Today the cave-riddled Bükk (beech) uplands are a convenient recreational area for the numerous inhabitants of a cluster of industrial towns, of which the most important is Miskolc, Hungary's second largest city. Even more extensive caves, some of the most spectacular in Europe, can be explored beneath the quiet countryside of the Aggteleki Hills on the Slovak frontier, while the easternmost Zemplén range shelters some of Hungary's best-preserved villages.

Looking south over the Great Plain from the final slopes of the mountains is a whole string of settlements, most of them conveniently linked to highway 3 and to the main Budapest–Miskolc–Kosice (Slovakia) railway line.

Just off the main communications route, but an essential stop on any itinerary are two places

*Bükk Mountain Nature Park*

of outstanding interest: the superb baroque town of Eger, and, further eastwards, Tokaj, both world famous for their wine.

◆
## BÜKK MOUNTAINS

The Bükk is best appreciated on foot, especially along the national 'Blue Route' or by climbing to the range's highest peak, Mount Istállós-kó (3,143 feet/958m). But drivers can get a good idea of the mountains by taking back roads from Eger to Miskolc.

The route northward from Eger passes through the village of Szarvaskö with its ruined castle, and close to the 13th-century abbey church at **Bélapátfalva.** Founded by Cistercian monks in 1232, this structure is that much-prized rarity in Hungary, an almost intact Romanesque church, somehow preserved from the ravages of time and Turk.

The forest resort of **Szilvásvárad** once belonged to the aristocratic Pallavicini family, whose taste for horsemanship is still reflected today in the Lippizaner stud, riding-track and equestrian museum. The family mansion is now a holiday home.

Szilvásvárad is the terminus for former forestry trains which chug along the narrow-gauge line leading up the pretty Szalajka Valley. The valley's attractions include fish ponds, a forest museum with displays evoking the life and work of woodmen and charcoal-burners, stepped waterfalls and caves. (See also page 92.)

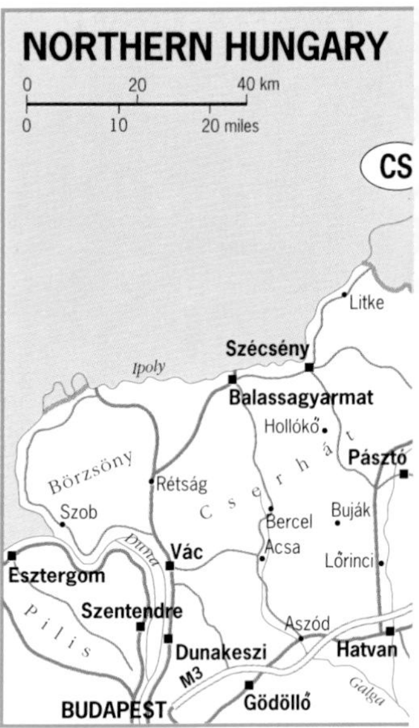


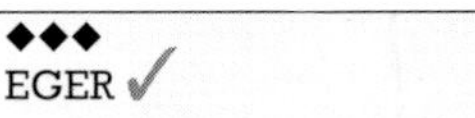

◆◆◆
## EGER ✓

Seen from the ramparts of its massive castle, the old city of Eger is obviously a gem of the baroque period, its roofscape adorned with the cupolas, belfries and turrets of churches and civic buildings. These emblems of the typical Central European city fit comfortably into the town's surroundings, cool forests and hills to the north, vineyards all around. But as the eye explores the pleasing panorama, an incongruous element probes the skyline. This is the bold minaret which once belonged to the city's chief mosque, a reminder that for nearly a century Eger was the capital of a Turkish province.

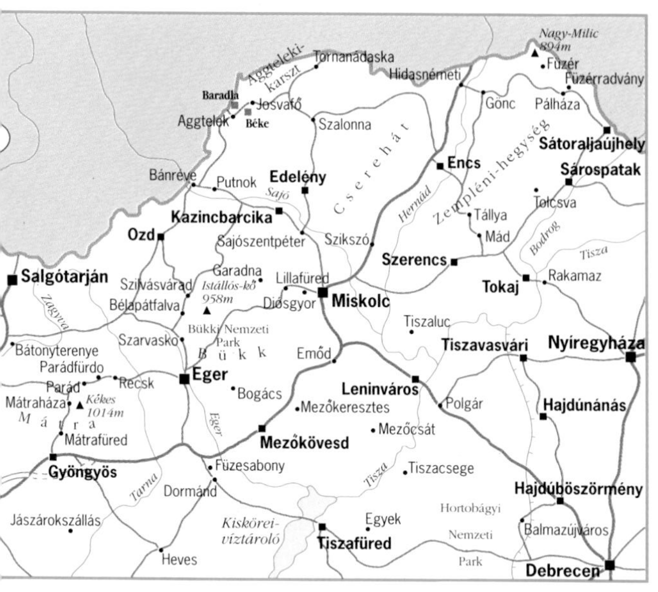


**A Hungarian hero**

Every Hungarian schoolchild is drilled in the epic resistance offered by Eger in 1552 to the seemingly unstoppable armies of the sultan. The castle's defence was commanded by Captain István Dobó. Against overwhelming odds, he and his small band of defenders, reinforced by the city's stalwart womenfolk, succeeded in driving off the besieging horde, giving all Europe a much-needed respite. The humiliation was all the greater when the castle later fell to the Turks almost without a fight.

Visitors may know the robust local red wine known as Egri Bikavér, or Bull's Blood.

Battered by the Turks, its ramparts blown up by the Habsburgs in 1702, enough of the castle survives to command the visitor's attention.

More of the castle's defences survive below ground (casemates, cannon chambers, underground barracks) than above, but the surviving walls and ramparts make a fine panoramic walk. They enclose a considerable area, containing the ruins of the **cathedral**, the **bishop's palace** (housing the castle museum, mint and Hall of Heroes), and a **picture gallery.**

The town itself offers any number of pleasing contrasts. The focal point is the spacious Dobó István tér, pedestrianised and completely dominated by the twin towers of St Anthony's, the modern department store

tactfully landscaped away. Fine buildings line the main streets, Kossuth utca and Széchenyi utca, which converge on the cold but enormously imposing cathedral and the huge building of the **Lyceum.** Ambitious Bishop Esterházy had this built in the late 18th century to house a university which failed to materialise. The interior is suitably grand, with a mind-reeling ceiling painting in the great library, while the observatory, in its mini-skyscraper, is worth visiting for the view and for its astronomical collection.

### Accommodation

It is quite feasible to make a hurried day trip to Eger from Budapest, but much more satisfactory to stay longer. The town has a good choice of hotels and those with the most character are:

**Szenátor-ház**, Dobó tér 11 (tel: 36/20 466), 3-star. At the top end of the town's main square, this is a small and comfortable hotel with an intimate atmosphere and a 'Turkish' café.

**Hotel Flóra**, Fürdö u 5 (tel: 36/20 211), 3-star. A large establishment in cheerful postmodern style, with its own thermal spring and spa facilities.

Among the pensions you could try **Panzió BB**, Gárdonyi u 43 (tel: 36/14 166), a family-run place with views over the city. English is claimed to be spoken and tours, including wine-tasting, can be arranged.

*Astronomy museum, Eger*

### Eating Out

**Talizmán**, Kossuth L u 23 (tel: 36/20 883). In an atmospheric semi-basement at the foot of the castle approach, with good local specialities.

**HBH Bavarian Beer Hall**, Bajcsy-Zsilinszky u 19 (tel: 36/16 312). HBH is short for Hofbräuhaus as in Munich, and here the ambience is Germanic, but the food is thoroughly Hungarian and good.

◆◆

## HOLLÓKÖ

In its hillside setting of orchards and overlooked by its ruined 13th-century castle, this is one of the best-preserved of Hungary's villages. It is much visited by tourists because it is one of the few places where traditional costume is still worn in a fairly spontaneous way, at least by its female inhabitants. The local people are members of the Palóc ethnic group, upland people of obscure origin distinguishable by their dialect and folk culture.

Since 1987 Hollókö has had the distinction of featuring on UNESCO's list of World Culture and Natural Heritage, and it is still one of the best places to get something of the 'feel' of Hungarian rural life of yesteryear.

The red-tiled houses are (or were) individual small farmsteads. Together with the wooden-towered church they compose an almost too-poignantly picturesque scene, enhanced by the animal noises (barks, grunts, clucks and baas) still emanating from some of the farmyards.

*The beauty of the Mátra mountains*

◆◆

## MÁTRA MOUNTAINS

The volcanically formed Mátra Mountains with their vast woodlands of beech and oak and abundant springs and streams, are Hungary's most popular recreational area after Balaton and Danube Bend. Here is Kékestetö, the country's highest peak at 3,330 feet (1,015m), whose excellent winter sunshine record brings skiers flocking to the pistes cut through the forest. In summer, the Mátra resorts are filled with city folk recovering from breathing Budapest air or curing their digestive problems at Páradfürdö's thermal spa. The usual approach to the mountains from Budapest is via the cheerful small town of **Gyöngyös,** which is also a handy place to stay. This industrial town is sited on the sunny south-facing slopes of the white-wine-producing Mátraalja vineyards. It boasts the country's largest Gothic church, **St Bartholemew's**, much baroquified in the 18th century, as well as the **Mátra Museum**, housed in the early 19th-century Orczy Mansion. The museum's exhibits cover every aspect of the region's history, from wildlife to wine-making. It is conveniently located next to the terminus of the narrow-gauge railway, the jolliest way of getting up to the mountain resort of **Mátrafüred**, though no further.

Beyond Mátrafüred and the lake at Sás is **Mátraháza**, lying at the foot of Kékestetö, with some of the best winter sports facilities in Hungary. The great **Telecommunications Tower** rising from the summit gives fantastic views in clear conditions, southward over the Great Plain and northward as far as the distant Tátras.

There are other resorts in the valleys threading the Mátras, most of them developed under the auspices of the Communist regime to provide guaranteed holidays for factory workers. The accommodation is thus mostly of the hostel type and not open to all comers, but there are a good number of private rooms available and there should be no difficulty in finding somewhere to stay.

The little spa at **Páradfürdö** has bubbly, sulphurous waters used in the treatment of digestive disorders. The place also has a coach and carriage museum; you probably did not realise that one of the very few words given to the world by the Hungarian language is 'coach', this kind of vehicle having been invented in Kocs (far away from here in Western Hungary – you should be able to guess how it is pronounced). In Párad itself is a preserved traditional village house, the **Palóc ház**, open to the public, its furnishings and fittings giving a very complete picture of the way of life of the local Palóc people (see also Hollókö, page 71).

### Accommodation, Food and Drink

**Gyöngyös**

**Mátra Hotel**, Mátyás király út 2 (tel: 37/12 057), 3-star. Right in the middle of town, this is a classic Central European hotel with restaurant, beer-cellar, café and comfortable rooms.

**Vinceller Panzio**, Erzsébet királynö u 22 (tel: 37/11 691). Conveniently located just off the road to the Mátras, this is a pleasant modern pension. Reductions apply if you stay more than three days. Welcoming restaurant with good range of meals including local specialities.

## MISKOLC

To the chagrin of its quarter of a million inhabitants, industrial Miskolc tends to get a bad press. It is a workaday place, with polluting factories, radial highways lined with high-rise flats and a city centre looking rather frayed at the edges, but few comparable industrial cities in Western Europe have a main street to match Miskolc's Széchenyi utca. Reserved for pedestrians and trams, this thoroughfare has an established air.

Away from this main artery are the fine twin-towered baroque **Church of the Minorites,** a Greek Orthodox church with a superb iconostasis, and one of the city's emblems, the wooden-towered **Reformed Church**, on the lower slopes of the Avas Hill. Topping the summit is Miskolc's modern emblem, the **TV tower** with a viewing platform enabling you to appreciate the full extent of Hungary's largest industrial city (excluding Budapest). The hill itself is riddled with the caves of wine-cellars, reminders of a once-flourishing wine trade.

One of Miskolc's attractions is

the spa in the suburb of Miskolc-Tapolca, where there are thermal baths and cave baths with a famous 'thrashing shower'.

**Excursions from Miskolc**

Miskolc's great asset is its position at the very edge of the woods and hills of the Bükk National Park. The main escape route from town is via the main highway westwards (or, alternatively, by narrow-gauge railway). The final suburb (formerly a place in its own right), is Diósgyör, where another one of the city's emblems, the fine four-towered **Queens' Castle** offers good views, and open-air concerts in summer.

The road continues mountainwards up the valley of the Szinva and arrives at the little resort of **Lillafüred** and artificial Lake Hámori. It is an open question whether the beautiful woodland setting is enhanced or not by the massive 1920s Palota Hotel. Lillafüred is known for its trio of limestone caves, as good an introduction as any to the sometimes spectacular effects of water on calcium carbonate.

Forest railway and highway accompany each other further up the Garadna valley towards the heart of the mountains. One stop *en route* is at a fine piece of industrial archaeology, the iron foundry built by the Fazola family early in the 19th century, now carefully preserved and with its own museum. The road continues beyond the terminus of the railway to connect with the forest road coming from the far side of the massif (see **Bükk Mountains**, page 68). Much further, about 43 miles (70km) away from Miskolc, among the wooded Aggtelek uplands are some of Europe's most spectacular caves. The **Baradla Cave** is 14 miles (22km) long; part of it extends over the nearby Czechoslovak frontier. To cross the border underground requires no passport but plenty of stamina for the nealy 6-hour walk through the entire length of the cave. Shorter tours can be made from the entrances at Jósvafö, Aggtelek (exhibition) and Vörös-tó. The **Béke** (Peace) **Caves**, only discovered in 1952, contain a chamber whose air is used to treat asthmatics.

**Accommodation**

Should you have to stay in Miskolc itself, the modern **Pannónia**, Kossuth L u 2 (tel: 46/16 434), 3-star, has the merit of being central (at the junction with Széchenyi u).

You might find the air fresher out of town in Lillafüred, where the **Palota** (Palace), built as a luxury hotel, converted postwar into a trade union hostel, is opening its doors to the public again. It has an extraordinary restaurant, with Gothic vaulting and stained-glass windows commemorating Hungary's 'lost' towns and castles. More modest quarters are to be found in the **Panzió Lilla,** Erzsébet sétány 7 (tel: 46/51 299), which makes every effort to be accommodating to its guests from abroad, with Hungarian home cooking and a photo-coded menu.

◆◆
## SÁROSPATAK

Bypassed by the main highway linking Hungary with eastern Slovakia and southern Poland, the small town of Sárospatak on the banks of the River Bodrog deserves to be better known to visitors from abroad. For Hungarians, however, Sárospatak and its surroundings have a high profile. It was in this border region that their tribal ancestors first settled after breaking through the barrier of the Carpathians, and Sárospatak's splendid **castle** has strong associations with the country's struggle for freedom from the Habsburgs.

The older part of the castle consists of a rugged keep in red sandstone known as the Red Tower, coexisting rather uneasily with the later, elegant fortified Renaissance mansion. Sárospatak itself contains the usual amenities of a Hungarian town of its size. The castle approach, Kata utca, is particularly pretty, with a big Gothic church at the corner and the former monastery which is now the Hotel Borostyán. In the main street is the old Calvinist **College**, testimony to the town's former cultural eminence, when, as a centre of humanist and Protestant learning, it was known – somewhat extravagantly – as 'Athens of the Bodrog'.

### Accommodation

Hotel and restaurant **Borostyán**, Kádár K u 28 (tel: 41/11 611), 2-star. Borostyán is housed in an old monastery, whose great hall has been converted into the town's best restaurant. Conveniently sited next to the castle. Behind the Borostyán is a large and famous wine-cellar, named like its counterpart in Tokaj after the great **Rákóczi.**

*Fantastic limestone formations in the Aggtelek caves*

## TOKAJ

Huddled at the foot of a high vine-clad hill at the meeting point of the Tisza and Bodrog rivers is the small community which has given its name to one of the world's great wines.

The Tokaj-Hegyalja region extends along the lower slopes of the Zemplén Hills. Its 13 square miles (50sq km) of vineyards are spread over the territory of 28 parishes, some of which (Mád, Tállya, Tolcsva) are famous wine villages in their own right. The vines flourish in the volcanic soil and because of the high level of sunshine, particularly in the autumn.

Fame came early to the wines of Tokaj – Tokay in English. Production may have begun as early as Celtic times, but it was from the Middle Ages onward that merchants came here from all over Europe to deal with the growing demand. Poland was the major destination of this trade, but Tokaj was a favourite of Louis XIV, who named it 'the wine of kings – the king of wines'. Another enthusiast was Peter the Great of Russia, who secured his personal supplies by buying up some of the vineyards, a process paralleled today as French interests take advantage of privatisation.

Tokaj is best seen in its setting from the far side of the bridge over the Tisza. The town itself has an air of faded charm. Most tourists head for the 17th-century **Rákóczi Cellar** with its mile (1½ km) of storage passageways and opportunities for sampling and buying. The cellar is worth seeing for its own sake – it was the scene of some of the events of the Rákóczi rebellion at the beginning of the 18th century – but there are plenty of other wine-cellars in and around Tokaj eager for your custom. Sober students of wine culture should head for the **Tokaj Museum** which traces the history of the grape hereabouts.

*The traditional vineyards at Tokaj have produced world-class wines for centuries*

## THE GREAT PLAIN

The sense of limitless space which the sea gives to maritime nations is found in Hungary in the Alföld, the 'Great Lowland' which stretches into infinite distances east of the Danube, its flat horizons sometimes interrupted only by the gaunt arm of a wooden water pump. Lazy watercourses meander slowly through the unrelieved flatness to join the region's great river, the Tisza.

Accounting for half the total area of present-day Hungary and often referred to as the *puszta*, this is where the waves of invading nomads from the steppes of Asia felt most at home, and where uniquely Hungarian landscapes and ways of life have developed.

Densely settled in the Middle Ages, the Great Plain was virtually depopulated in Turkish times. The countryside degenerated into pestilential swamplands, inhabited only by brigands and swineherds, the rest of the population clustering for safety in a small number of towns. Some of these were no more than overgrown villages, others like Debrecen and Kecskemét were able to satisfy the occupiers' demand for tribute and continued to flourish.

On the departure of the Turks, the area was repopulated by the Habsburgs, with fewer Magyars who were such a thorn in their flesh than with the more pliant Germans, Slovaks, Rumanians, Serbs and Jews. These added to an already colourful racial mix, composed not only of Magyars but also of descendants of other nomadic peoples; Cumanians and Jazygians as well as Gypsies and the independent warrior caste known as Hayduks.

Draining the swamps and taming the rivers led to the spread of great stretches of grassland and the supremacy of the herdsman's way of life. This culture, subsequently much romanticised, with its emphasis, like the Wild West's, on horsemanship and tough self-sufficiency, began to decline in the late 19th century, together with the landscape which gave rise to it.

To begin with, great landowners, then their successors the State Farm managers, found it more profitable to grow grain, fruit and vines. The *puszta* and its denizens do live on, however, carefully preserved in the national parks at Hortobágy and Bugac, a 'must' on any tourist itinerary.

By its very nature, the Great Plain is monotonous, particularly when seen from the window of a train or express coach. Do not expect conventionally picturesque scenes. The countryside's appeal often lies in the particular rather than the general: a tiny *tanya*, a scruffy smallholding, with its array of animals, water pump and tumbledown cottage alone in the middle of a vast field, a seemingly deserted village suddenly coming to life as parishioners pour out of church in their Sunday best, an ancient biplane on an isolated airstrip.

## DEBRECEN

Debrecen has the air of a big city about it: trams glide along the middle of the broad main street, Piac (Market) utca, which is lined by large modern buildings and ends at the dignified façade of the great Reformed Church. Indeed, Debrecen is Hungary's second most populous city after Budapest, having recently pushed industrial Miskolc into third place.

However, close to Piac utca are streets of single-storey houses with great arched doorways leading into courtyards and gardens. The crowds here no longer consist of metropolitan sophisticates but rather of countryfolk, heading homewards from the huge covered market (one of the country's best), perhaps with a live goose in a plastic bag.

**Protestant stronghold**

This city of contrasts used to be known as the 'Calvinist Rome'. One of the great strongholds of Protestantism, it held out doggedly against both Turks (with tributes of money) and Counter-Reformation (with faith). Its importance in national life was enhanced in 1849, when the Hungarian government declared its (short-lived) independence from the Habsburgs here, and again in 1944, when the (slightly longer-lived) Provisional National Government was set up under the auspices of the liberating Red Army.

The twin towers of the **Reformed Church** in Piac utca were set as far apart as they are in order to accommodate a dome which was never built. Dating from 1805–27, the church is even more austere inside than out, a stern warning against the baroque frivolities

so prevalent elsewhere in this largely Catholic country. It was within these white walls that Kossuth assembled his countrymen to hurl defiance against the Habsburg tyrant. Behind the church is Debrecen's other great Protestant monument, the **Calvinist College**, a sober, classical-style, early 19th-century building, and a venue for both the nationalist revolutionaries of 1849 and the soon-to-be-deluded democrats of 1944. The faces of the latter appear in one of the exhibits of the nearby **Déri Museum**, in

the section dealing with the city's history. This part is interesting enough for those with a ready knowledge of Hungarian. However, the other main sections are much more accessible to the visitor – Archaeology, Ethnography, Art and History.

### Accommodation

**Hotel Arany Bika** (Golden Bull), Piac u 11–15 (tel: 52/16 777), 3-star. With restaurants (including a brasserie), a charming patisserie, night club and huge foyer, it is a city institution and meeting place. Its bedroom windows give on to Piac utca and the main façade of the Reformed Church.

Even if you are unable to afford a night here, at least eat in the main restaurant, with its bright décor and high glazed roof.

**Hotel Fönix**, Barna u 17 (tel: 52/13 355), 3-star, competes with the Arany Bika less on allure than on price and almost equally central location.

### Eating Out

**Gambrinus**, Piac u 28. Good Hungarian food and German beer, to the accompaniment of violin and cimbalom.

**Csokonai**, Kossuth u. Debrecen's prosperous younger generation queue to eat beneath the atmospheric brick vaults of this cellar restaurant. Useful pictorial menu in English and German.

## GYULA

Just short of the frontier, on one of the highways linking Hungary with Romania, this leafy little town is not only a useful staging post for long-distance travellers but a destination in its own right for the thousands who hope to cure their ills at its modern spa.

The town's main sight is its formidable red-brick medieval **castle**, flanked by a quaint

*The façade of the Calvinist College commemorates Zwingli and Calvin, the famous religious reformers*

round tower. Its survival more or less intact through the troubled times of Turkish invasion and occupation makes it a great rarity in this part of Hungary, all the more appreciated during the summer festival season when performances and concerts take place within its sturdy walls.
Gyula is proud of its associations with the great German Renaissance painter Dürer (whose father hailed from here), and with Ferenc Erkel (born here in 1810), composer of patriotic operas and the Hungarian national anthem. In the square named after him, Erkel tér, is the **Százéves Cukrászda**, the 'Century Café', its interior a delight of pale chocolate and crème de menthe décor and Biedermeier furniture. A tiny museum at the back of the café displays the tools of the pastrycook's trade. Outside are two of the town's baroque churches, one Protestant, one Catholic. An ecclesiastical interior worth inspecting is that of the **Greek Orthodox Church**, close to the spa.

### Accommodation

As befits a spa town, there is a fair choice of hotels, including the very reasonably priced **Erkel Hotel** or the **Aranykereszt**, both near the spa. Outside town at Mezöhegyes (tel: 69/11 045) is the 3-star **Hotel Nonius**, part of a country estate offering rural programmes of all kinds (such as hunting and riding), as well as a carriage museum.

◆◆◆
## HORTOBÁGY NATIONAL (NEMZETI) PARK ✓

For generations of Central Europeans, the Great Plain was an almost unimaginably exotic place, a boundless grassy expanse inhabited by strangely garbed herdsmen and their animals, living not in villages but in temporary shelters of reed and straw.
Haunted in midsummer by strange mirages, the plain is blasted in winter by icy winds howling down from the Carpathians. The way of life here until fairly recently was indeed almost unique, its preoccupation with horsemanship and its lack of settled culture evoking something of the spirit of the steppes from which the ancient Magyars sprang.
This seemingly primeval landscape began to disappear in the 19th century, when the River Tisza was tamed by engineering works, and no longer enriched the grassland with its annual floodwaters. More recently, grass has given way to croplands, reducing the original area of *puszta* to a few fragments, albeit sizeable ones. Hortobágy, at 243 square miles (630sq km), is the largest of these. Preserved as a national park since 1973, it is approached via the fast highway no 33, the great fields of maize and other crops giving way to a more unkempt scene. Interspersed with reedbeds and willow groves are vast sweeps of grassland, grazed here and there by sheep and

long-horned cattle with attendant herdsmen. The signs warning you to keep away bring home the realisation that this is a stage-managed scene, carefully controlled by the administrators of the national park, not just for the entertainment of the visitor, but in order to preserve the unique character of the landscape.

You can penetrate the mysteries of the *puszta* in a number of ways. The easiest and jolliest is to join the crowds at Hortobágy itself. Here is the famous nine-arched stone bridge (the longest one in Hungary) over the Hortobágy River and the even more famous *csárda* (**Nagycsárda**), as well as any number of kiosks offering a variety of 'Programmes'. The choice includes carriage rides, visits to the various herds, virtuoso displays of horsemanship and whip-cracking. You can bring the day to an end with a folklore display and bacon roasting by the campfire. The atmosphere in the *csárda*, a fine long white building with an arcaded gallery, is likely to become very cheery as the evening wears on. (See also **Peace and Quiet**, page 91.)

## KALOCSA

Burned down during the Turkish occupation and abandoned by the Danube (now four miles (6km) to the west), this small town has nevertheless kept its three big claims to fame. The seat of an archbishop (second in rank only to the Primate of Esztergom) with a fine baroque cathedral and archbishop's palace, it also enjoys a nationwide reputation for its paprika and for the arts and crafts of its inhabitants.

The archbishops have been here since very early days and the bishopric was established by King Stephen in the 11th century. The reigning archbishop was felled by a Turkish sword at the Battle of Mohács in 1526. But the Turkish invasion brought benefits as well as bother, chief among them the paprika pepper which makes Hungarian cooking so distinctive. The plant thrives in the hot sun hereabouts. You can see it growing in the countryside around the town or hung out to dry on the white walls of village houses, and you can even study its history in what must be the world's only **Paprika Museum**.

The 'painting women' of Kalocsa have a long tradition of using colourful floral motifs in the decoration not only of clothes and linen, but also of house interiors, together with their furnishings. Their work can be seen in both the **Viski Károly Museum** and in the **Népmü vészeti Ház** (Folk Art House), while even the waiting room in Kalocsa railway station has been given the floral treatment!

◆◆

## KECSKEMÉT

Urban centre for the vast and rich farmlands extending from the Danube to the Tisza, Kecskemét's long-standing prosperity is reflected in the splendid buildings which grace its spacious squares. Your appreciation of the peculiarly Hungarian contribution to Art Nouveau architecture will not be complete without a visit here. Its extravagances are sometimes less digestible than the fiery spirit distilled from the apricots grown in abundance around the town, the famous *Kecskeméti barackpálinka* (apricot brandy).

Kecskemét managed to thrive even under Turkish rule, when country-dwellers settled here for protection. But its boom times really began as the countryside prospered again at the end of the 19th century and its agricultural products flowed into town to be processed and marketed.

The profits from all this activity seem to have been spent wisely, on public buildings like the huge **Town Hall** of 1893–6 in Kossuth tér, a flamboyant attempt to create a distinctively Hungarian style of building. In front of it is a great block of stone, split asunder, with the inscription 'One of Kecskemét's greatest sons broke his heart here'. This commemorates the death (by heart attack) of the great playwright **József Katona** (1791–1830), whose other memorial is the grandiose and beautifully restored municipal theatre named after him.

Kecskemét's other great son, better known internationally than Katona and fortunately much longer-lived, was **Zoltán Kodály** (1882–1967), inspiring composer (*Háry János*) and even more inspiring teacher of music. The **Kodály Institute of Music Teaching** has a fine home in the cloisters of the old Franciscan Monastery, in the pretty pedestrian street just off the square.

Kossuth tér too has been attractively pedestrianised and landscaped. Together with Szabadság (Freedom) tér, it forms a leafy setting for the places of worship which cluster here in convivial tolerance, from the classical **Roman Catholic Church** of 1806 near the town hall, via the baroque former **Church of the Franciscans** and the much rebuilt **Reformed Church,** to the exotic late-19th-century **Synagogue** (now a 'House of Technology') closing the vista with its onion dome. Close by

*Kecskemét's Cifra Palace*

are the square's most remarkable buildings, the massive Transylvanian-style **New College** of 1911 and the extraordinary **Cifra palota** (Ornamental Palace), built in 1902. These architectural delights are hard to top, but the town also has its share of museums. The one named after Katona houses the local history collection, but you might be more intrigued by the **Museum of Hungarian Naive Art** or the **Szórakaténusz Toy Workshop and Museum** which is housed in a cheerful modern building and is happy to let visiting children play with its toys.

### Excursion from Kecskemét

BUGAC-PUSZTA

Southwest of Kecskemét lies a vast area of grasslands and sand dunes. Part of the **Kiskunság National (Nemzeti) Park**, it is a preserved landscape like the Hortobágy, home to the rare breeds of animal which grazed the Great Plain before most of it was ploughed up to produce its crops of grain, fruit and vines. It is an evocative, almost elemental place, somewhat aside from the main communication routes, and it is perhaps here that you can best catch a glimpse of the way of life of the herdsmen and 'cowboys' who once ranged the *puszta*.

The last stage of the approach to Bugac, past a number of *tanyas* with old breeds of chickens, ducks and geese pecking away in their yards, must be made on foot or by horse and cart. The great grassy tract is grazed by beasts you are unlikely to have seen before – wide-horned Podolian cattle from the steppes or curly-horned Racka sheep. The stables house half-bred (bay, yellow and cream) horses, and there are spectacular displays of horsemanship (in which you may be invited to participate!) in front of the **Pásztormúzeum** (Herdsmen's Museum). This yurt-like building has a fascinating array of objects once used by the herdsmen in their daily life and work.

Beyond the grassland, and accessible only with special permission from the National Park Administration, is a wild area of wetlands and sand dunes, the 'highlands' of the Great Plain, with rare flora and fauna.

Easier to get into is the **Bugaci csárda**, as atmospheric as the *puszta* itself, where the folk music seems especially

*Elegant spire on a village church*

authentic and the goulash particularly filling!

**Accommodation**
Two establishments offer you rooms in the centre of Kecskemét, one large and modern (well, 1960s modern), the **Aranyhomok**, Széchenyi tér 3 (tel: 76/20 011), 3-star; the other, the **Három Gúnár** (Three Ganders), Batthyány u 1 (tel: 76/27 077), in a restored old building. Off the Budapest road to the north of the town there is a small country hotel, the **Gerébi**, with chalets as well (Alsólajos 224, tel: 76/56 045).

**Eating Out**
The stylish place to meet and eat not over-expensively in Kecskemét is in the immaculate surroundings of the **Café Szabadság** or **Liberté** conveniently situated in the centre of the town's pedestrianised squares.
*End of excursion*

◆◆
## SZEGED
A university city, regional capital of the southern part of the Great Plain, Szeged once nearly disappeared from the map. In 1879, the mighty River Tisza burst its banks and engulfed the city, destroying all but a few buildings. Rebuilding took place quickly, on new, rational lines. A central grid pattern of streets and squares was encircled by two ring boulevards. The outer one commemorates the capitals of the countries which contributed to Szeged's reconstruction (including London, Paris, Berlin, and Vienna). Because of the speed of rebuilding, the city's architectural character is unusually harmonious, with many fine examples of late 19th-century building at its best. Standing out from the greys and pastels of the inner city is the resolutely reddish-brown brick **Votive Church**, a twin-towered architectural extravaganza built to celebrate Szeged's rebirth after the flood, but only completed in 1929. It forms a dramatic background to the performances held in the cathedral square during the city's Summer Festival (20 July to 20 August), watched from tiered terrace seating. The arcades around the square form a Hungarian Hall of Fame, with busts of the famous attached to their walls. Further pomp awaits just to the south, where trams swish through the huge arcaded 'Heroes Gate', guarded by stern stone soldiers.

The everyday focus of the town is **Széchenyi tér**, more of a park than a square, with statuary celebrating the blessings and misfortunes conferred by the Tisza. Between the trees rises the tower of the **Town Hall,** a cheerful exercise in neo-baroque and an early commission for the great Art Nouveau architect, Ödön Lechner. There are a number of fine examples of the Art Nouveau style, none more flamboyant that the **Reök Palace** with its luxuriant water-lily decoration inside and out (corner of Kosey u and Bajcsy-Zsilinszky u).

The city's real architectural gem, however, is the **New**

**Synagogue**, built in 1903 by Szeged's once prosperous Jewish community. Externally impressive enough, it is the synagogue's interior which surprises and delights, above all because of its stained-glass dome, a structure of unbelievable delicacy and intensity of colour (key from the Jewish old people's home in Jókai u).

Modern Szeged has rather turned its back on the Tisza and overlooks the river from a sensibly high promenade, below which traffic races along in Parisian fashion. Not quite all of old Szeged was swept away in the flood and some of the modest streets in the **Lower Town** (Alsóváros) are a reminder of pre-1879 days. In Mátyás Király tér is the **Franciscans' Church**, whose gorgeously lavish baroque altar contrasts with sober Gothic vaulting.

### Accommodation

Szeged has two hotels belonging to the Hungar chain: the **Royal**, Kölcsey u 1 (tel: 62/12 911), 2-star, and the **Hungária**, Komocsin Zoltán tér (tel: 62/21 211), 3-star. The former is older, hemmed in among the streets of the city centre, the latter modern, on the edge of the centre overlooking the Tisza. In spite of the different star rating, rooms are the same price at both establishments.

Of the city's several private pensions, **Pölös Attila**, in Pacsirta u 17/A (tel: 62/27 974) is fairly close to town, while the popular **Marika** in Nyíl u 45 (tel: 62/13 861) is in the southwestern suburbs.

### Eating Out

The **Hungária's** plush restaurant boasts of its local specialities, but these can be sampled more cheaply in the cheerful atmosphere of the cluster of fish restaurants a mile or so upstream (best reached by taxi). This is where locals gather to enjoy Szeged's famous fish soup: fiery with paprika, this memorable dish nevertheless goes well with the good white wine of the region, Pusztamergési rizling. At the **Kiskörös Halászcsárda** you can dance to the international repertoire of a multilingual university professor on synthesizer.

*The rural charm of the Great Plain*

# *Peace and Quiet*

*Wildlife and Countryside in Hungary by Paul Sterry*

Mountains, marshes, forests, lakes and remnants of the Great Plain (Alföld) all contribute to the diversity of Hungary's landscapes. Since the country is quite small – only 300 miles (483km) across and 150 miles (241km) deep – this makes for lots of variety.

In a country that is still largely rural, there are many opportunities to explore quiet, beautiful countryside; the areas listed below have been chosen for their intrinsic qualities, and for the wealth of wildlife that can be seen. Many of these places have visitor facilities.

## In and Around Budapest

For those visitors to Budapest who would like a break from city life, there are several sites within easy reach of the centre.

**Margaret Island** (Margit-sziget) lies in the middle of the Danube river, where it cuts the city in two. This is essentially a recreational area, with a theatre and swimming pool among its attractions. However, there are tranquil wooded stretches with the added bonus of plenty of birds to look out for. In particular, Syrian woodpeckers are often found among the trees, and migrant collared flycatchers also nest here in the spring. They are small, active birds which feed among the higher branches and have striking black-and-white plumage.

**Városliget** (The City Park) is also an extremely good spot for woodland birds. Spring is the best time of year, when resident and newly-arrived migrant species will be singing.

The best spot for relaxing walks and observing wildlife in the vicinity of Budapest is the **Buda Hills** (Budai-hegység) which are located to the west of the city and, in part, within its boundaries. There are regular bus services to the hills, and a chair lift operates to the highest point – Janos-hegy – from Zugliget. The hills are heavily wooded and, not surprisingly, are good for birds such as woodpeckers. In summer, look and listen for several species of warblers which nest here.

## Lake Velence (Valencei-tó)

Lake Velence lies 31 miles (50km) southwest of Budapest and is about 6 miles (10km) long and 2 miles (3km) wide. Velence itself lies at the northeast corner of the lake and can be reached from the capital either by taking the M7, which runs along the northwestern shores of the lake, or route 70, which runs along the south-eastern shores. There is also a train service from Budapest to Gárdony or Dinnyés on the southern shores of the lake. Most of the shoreline can be explored from tracks and roads around the lake.

The eastern shoreline is popular with tourists and visitors and so has less wildlife than the western and northern shores of the lake. In undisturbed areas, however, birdlife is abundant on the open water and in the reedbeds that fringe many areas of this shallow lake. The **Dinnyés Marshes**, around the village of the same name, are a nature reserve for which prior permission is needed to enter. However, a vast array of birdlife can be seen by exploring tracks from the village. Almost any pond, marshy field or reedbed will have something to see.

During the summer months, look in marshy fields for birds such as white storks, which breed in many of the villages, and waders such as ruff and godwits. Herons breed in the reedbeds along with warblers, harriers, bearded tits and numerous other water birds. Frogs and toads are also abundant – although more easily heard than seen.

During spring and autumn, large numbers of migrant birds pass through the region. Look for wildfowl and grebes on the open water, terns hawking for insects over the marshes and waders, egrets and herons in the shallows.

**White stork**

Many country villages and towns in Hungary have white storks nesting on their rooftops and chimneys. The birds are usually oblivious to the presence of people and are often actively encouraged to build their large and untidy nests. This is because storks are thought to confer good fortune on those households they choose to nest on. The birds feed on frogs, fish and insects and can often be seen feeding in fields and meadows close to villages. They are summer visitors to Europe, heading south in the autumn to spend the winter in Africa.

### Lake Balaton

Continuing southwest on the M7 from Budapest, the visitor eventually approaches Lake Balaton, central Europe's largest freshwater lake. Roads run around almost the entire shoreline and, during the summer months, this is an extremely busy tourist resort. The lake can also be reached by railway from Budapest – the line runs along the northern shore.

Not surprisingly, much of the shore adjacent to resort towns is effectively devoid of wildlife interest. However, there are several sites where this is not the case and these are worth exploring even at the height of summer. Outside the main tourist season, there is less disturbance to the open water and margins and, during these times, large numbers of migrant and wintering wildfowl and other water birds can be seen. **Tihany** is an undulating peninsula on the northern shore of the lake southwest of Balatonfüred. The town is linked to Budapest by rail and there are buses and ferries to Tihany itself. There are plenty of opportunities for walks inland through farmland, woodland and around Tihany's two lakes. The bays on both sides of the peninsula are worth scanning with binoculars during the autumn and winter months, for a sight of ducks, geese and grebes.

At the southernmost part of Lake Balaton lies an internationally important wetland reserve called **Kis-Balaton** (Little Balaton). Marshes have formed on either side of the River Zala, which feeds the lake. They are roughly 6 miles (10km) south of Keszthely, the nearest villages being Balatonszentgyörgy and Zalavár. Most of the reserve can only be entered with prior permission and in any case is effectively inaccessible because of the nature of the terrain. However, observation towers are open to the public and give views of wetland birds.

### Bakony Hills

These picturesque hills, to the north of Lake Balaton, offer splendid opportunities for walking among superb scenery of rocky outcrops, river and wooded slopes. The towns of Veszprém, Tapolca and Sümeg make good bases from which to explore the area. Beechwoods, in particular, should be searched for interesting woodland flowers such as helleborines and yellow birdnest, while birdlife includes several species of woodpeckers as well as warblers and flycatchers. Veszprém can be reached from Budapest by taking the M7 as far as Székesfehérvár and then route 8. The town of Zirc, some 15 miles (24km) north of Veszprem on route 82, has an excellent arboretum with superb lime trees and conifers. Woodland birds, including hawfinches, are often easy to see.

*The white stork in flight*

**Kiskunság National Park**

Sadly, most of the original grasslands that comprised Hungary's Great Plain – the *puszta* – have disappeared, having been replaced by agricultural land. But open vistas do still remain and there are still a few meadows full of flowers, as well as marshes and lakes of varying importance to wildlife. Fortunately, six of the best remnant pockets of natural habitat have been preserved and together comprise the Kiskunság National (Nemzeti) Park.

Kecskemét is the best starting point for exploring the area; the town can be reached by driving south from Budapest on route 5. There is also a train service to the town. From there, head west and explore the area of land within the triangle formed by Kecskemét, Kiskóros and Kunszentmiklós.

Areas of natural grassland will hold flowers such as spiked speedwell, wild liquorice, corn marigold and many others, with an abundance of insects such as field crickets. Birdlife of these open areas includes red-footed falcons and rollers, both of which habitually perch on overhead wires.

Perhaps of more interest to the birdwatcher will be the lakes, marshes and reedbeds of the area. The best spots include Lake Kolon (Kolon-tó), southwest of Izák, and soda lakes west of Szabadszállás and Fulöpszállás. The best seasons are spring and autumn – April to May and August to September – when a wide range of waders and terns can be seen. Several species of herons and warblers breed in the reedbeds that fringe many of the pools. Look for a large black-and-yellow spider called Argiope among the vegetation.

*Look carefully for the Common Tree Frog, which has vivid green and brown skin, blending easily with the foliage*

**Penduline Tits**
Few birds are as endearing as these; they are most commonly associated with willows and other trees that grow in marshy ground and along wet ditches. Adult birds are easily recognised by their chestnut backs, grey heads and distinctive black 'masks'. In the spring, they build beautiful woven nests, shaped like flasks, that are suspended from a slender branch. Outside the breeding season, they roam around in sizeable flocks and can be located by their high-pitched call.

### Ócsa Forest

Lying less than 19 miles (30km) southeast of Budapest, this interesting and varied reserve area is easily reached from the capital. Although the reserve proper – marshy woodland – can only be entered with prior permission, the forest and adjacent meadows are easily viewed from the roads between Ócsa and Dabas to the southeast, or Ócsa and Bugyi to the southwest. Look for white storks feeding in the meadows alongside breeding waders, including redshank and snipe. Birds of prey sometimes soar overhead from the woodland, so stop and scan the skies from time to time. Frogs and insects are abundant in the wet ditches.

### Hortóbagy

Lying in eastern Hungary, the Hortóbagy is the best remaining area of the *puszta* which comprised the Great Hungarian Plain (Alföld). In addition to the steppe-like habitat of flower-rich grassland that is characteristic of the *puszta*, there are also lakes, woodlands and areas of marshes. Now a national park, the rural lifestyle and culture of the *puszta* peasants is protected. Many parts of the Hortóbagy have probably changed little in appearance for centuries and so retain much of their wildlife interest.

The focal point of the national park is Hortóbagy village, 22 miles (35km) west of Debrecen on route 33. Here there is a national park exhibition and museum celebrating the life of the *puszta*. Hortóbagy is well known for its nine-holed bridge which is at the centre of the annual horse show and fairs. Here, too, you can arrange for a guide to accompany you on visits to some of the protected parts of the national park.

Although the marshes of the Hortóbagy are largely inaccessible because of the nature of the terrain, the open steppe grassland can be viewed from tracks and roads radiating from Hortóbagy village. Indeed, a car can serve the additional purpose of acting as a mobile hide, thus allowing good views of otherwise nervous birds. Specialities of the grassland areas include the great bustards – among the largest birds in the world capable of fight – tawny pipits, short-toed larks and red-footed falcons.

Needless to say, the steppe grassland is alive with insects during the summer months. Grasshoppers and

bush-crickets abound and butterflies are frequent visitors to the numerous flowers. Susliks – burrowing mammals rather like hamsters – live in underground burrows and share this lifestyle with field crickets, males of which 'sing' from the entrance to their burrow in the spring.
Large numbers of small lakes – in reality most are actually fishponds – are found east of Hortóbagy. Many can be viewed easily from roads and tracks, and visitors should look out for terns and waders, particularly during spring and autumn migration. Large numbers of herons, egrets, spoonbills, warblers and crakes breed among the wetland vegetation, and grebes and ducks can be seen on the open water. The healthy populations of fish as well as amphibians help sustain their numbers. During the late autumn, large numbers of white-fronted geese arrive to spend the winter here.

### Aggtelek Mountains (Aggtelek karszt)

The villages of Aggtelek and Josvafo lie at either end of one of the most spectacular and extensive cave systems in Europe, famous for its stalactite and stalagmite formations. In addition to geological attractions, the Aggtelek Mountains – much now within a national park – offer superb limestone karst scenery with extensive, mature forests. There are plenty of opportunities for walking in the Aggtelek Mountains, and a nature trail links the Aggtelek and Josvafo entrances of the cave system. When walking in the hills, look for birds of prey (including golden eagles) soaring overhead, and woodpeckers among the trees. Several species of orchids are commonly seen growing on the woodland floor in summer.

### Bükk National (Nemzeti) Park

The Bükk Mountains lie close to the Slovak border, about 93 miles (150km) from Budapest. These limestone mountains, nearly 40,000 hectares of which comprise a national park, are cloaked in forest and offer streams, waterfalls, caves and gorges to explore.

**Woodland Orchids**

Limestone soils, even those covered in forest, can be extremely good for orchids, and the limestone plateau of the Bükk Mountains is no exception to this. Orchids are shrouded in mystery and always arouse interest in botanists. One reason for this is that it takes many years after a seed has germinated to produce a new flowering plant. Successful germination and growth depends on an underground association with a fungus to ensure survival. Consequently, many species of orchid are rather elusive. In woodland clearings in the Bükk Mountains, look for military orchids and lady orchids, while in deep shade, several species of helleborines grow.

**Woodpeckers**

One of the most characteristic groups of birds in Hungary's woodlands are the woodpeckers. They range in size from the tiny lesser-spotted woodpecker to the crow-sized black woodpecker. All share the ability to climb well, having their toes arranged for this purpose, and all habitually feed using their powerful bills to drill holes in rotting wood or to lift bark in search of insects. Woodpeckers nest in trees and most species excavate a hole specially for this purpose. Spring is the best season to look for them, since at this time of year, males will be calling loudly and 'drumming' by tapping their bills on branches to advertise their presence in a territory.

A limestone plateau, roughly 12 miles (20km) long and 3 miles (5km) wide, is at the heart of the Bükk Mountains. Its elevation is mostly between 800 and 900 metres, the highest points being Bálvány at 956 metres and Istálló-skö at 958 metres. From Eger, there is a winding mountain road to Miskolc, a good base from which to explore. Other mountain bases include Lillafüred and Szilvásvárad, which can be reached from Miskolc by bus. Numerous trails lead through the forest and access is open. One trail, from the village of Szilvásvárad, passes through the Szalajka Valley to the Istálló-skö Caves and is particularly rewarding.

The most characteristic forest tree in the Bükk Mountains is the beech, which grows particularly well on limestone soil. When the beech trees grow close together, they cast such a dense shade that comparatively few plants grow on the woodland floor. The flora and fauna is generally more diverse on slopes and beside streams where more light can penetrate. These are often the best areas to look for woodland birds and flowers.

*The great-spotted woodpecker perches proudly on his newly ventilated tree trunk*

**Szeged**

Set 109 miles (175km) south of Budapest, Szeged makes a good base from which to explore southern Hungary. It can be reached by driving south from the capital on route 5 or by taking a train. The River Tisza flows through the middle of Szeged and is itself of considerable wildlife interest away from the town. Perhaps of more interest, however, are the lakes and fishponds that can be found in the surrounding countryside:

**Lake Péteri** (Péteri-tó) lies between Szeged and Kecskemét, 9 miles (15km) south of Kiskunfélegyháza and on the west side of the road (route 5). An information centre, trails and observation platforms all help to make the lake easy to explore and understand. The main wildlife interest is birds and visitors should look for herons, egrets, ducks and terns around the lake itself.

**Lake Fehér** (Féher-tó) is another area of wetland comprising mainly fishponds and reedbeds. It lies on the eastern side of route 5 north of Szeged. There is a public observation platform, but most of the area is a reserve and requires a permit.

**Hanság**

The Hanság lies in northwest Hungary and is part of the Great Hungarian Plain (Alföld). Although changes in land use, modern agricultural practices and drainage have affected the area greatly, it still contains elements of the flora and fauna of these once vast steppe grasslands. Here, visitors can find expansive meadows, small pockets of woodland and the inevitable fishponds. As an added bonus, the southern end of Austria's Neusiedler See – in Hungary called Lake Fertö – is close at hand.

The Hanság, which is contiguous with the Tadten Plain in eastern Austria, is best explored by driving along the roads and tracks between Mosonmagyaróvár and Kapuvár to the south. Almost anywhere is likely to hold wildlife interest. Patches of willow scrub along wet ditches will hold penduline tits, red-backed shrikes and golden orioles, while the open plains are home to a few great bustards. Montagu's harriers regularly quarter the fields in search of small mammals, and white storks frequent the wet ditches in search of frogs. To explore Lake Fertö, take minor roads heading east from Sopron.

*The delicate spiked speedwell*

# *Practical*

*This section (with the yellow band) includes food, drink, shopping, accommodation, nightlife, tight budget, special events etc.*

## FOOD AND DRINK

### Eating

You are unlikely to go hungry in Hungary! Adjectives like hearty, rich, satisfying come to mind when trying to evoke the highly individual qualities of what is one of the world's most distinctive cuisines.

The Hungarian dish everyone has heard of is, of course, goulash (*gulyás*). The origins of this classic dish go back a thousand years, to the days when the herdsmen roamed the great plains carrying their supplies of food with them. Even today, you may find that your most memorable goulash was the one prepared in a great cauldron in the open air in somewhere like the *csárdas* in the Bugac National Park. There are many dishes bearing the name goulash, but the basic (and some say the best) goulash is made from cubes of beef cooked with onions and potatoes, perhaps with tomatoes, peppers and garlic, and always with caraway seeds as well as that other important ingredient of Hungarian cooking, paprika powder.

**Paprika**

Paprika – red pepper – is not native to Hungary. Although no-one is quite sure where it originated, it is quite possible that it was introduced (like coffee) by the Turks. There are several varieties, mostly sweet rather than sharp; it is a rich source of vitamin C – perhaps just as well in view of the relative absence from the restaurant menus of fresh fruit and vegetables. There is a unique Paprika museum at Kalocsa (see page 82).

Less well known than goulash are three other nourishing stews containing paprika: *Pörkölt* tends to have a thicker consistency and can be made from virtually any meat, though veal is normal, while *paprikas* is similar but with the addition of cream. The beef or veal used in the dish known as *tokany* is cut into strips; the meat is accompanied by vegetables like asparagus, peas and mushrooms, and sour cream is added.

Other meaty delights include spicy sausages from Debrecen,

smoked Gyulai sausages, and the world's finest salami (still a bargain, and an excellent, if not enduring souvenir!). Geese are widely eaten, most prized (and force-fed) for their liver. If your conscience permits, this is a product not to be missed, perhaps best of all roasted in its own fat.

The delicious gravies yielded by these heavy dishes are made heavier still by their normal accompaniment of various forms of pasta; these include *tarhonya* (pellets of dough), *galuska* (dumplings) or *csipetke* (noodles). A lighter element is supplied in the form of a side salad, not one of the triumphs of the Hungarian table, consisting of gherkins, peppers and grated cabbage. The humble cabbage receives a more respectful treatment when presented stuffed, usually with a mixture of minced pork and rice, while another vegetable dish which can be a meal in itself is the famous *lescö*, consisting of peppers, tomatoes, onions and bacon fried in pork fat.

In this inland country, lake and river fish like carp and perch have a status which those used to a good supply of ocean fare may find difficult to fully appreciate. Balaton *fogas* (pike-perch) is almost boneless, but beware the bones beneath the surface of some varieties of fish stew!

The main course in a Hungarian meal is followed by a dessert of equal richness, thin pancakes (*palacsinta*) with various fillings (nuts, poppy seeds, chocolate sauce, fruit, cream and sour cream) or strudels (*rétes*) vying with Vienna's best. A fresh fruit salad is unlikely and cheese is generally undistinguished.

International cuisine (normally Germanic) is increasingly available, if expensive, in restaurants, but if price is a problem – and this is a country

***Tastefully displayed fruit***

where it is possible to eat quite expensively – remember you can live very cheaply. Take the risk and follow the crowd to the sausage kiosk or the self-service buffet, or buy your picnic ingredients in shops and markets (the best source for excellent fresh fruit, especially the delicious sour cherries). Look out for snacks like corn on the cob sold on the street. It is always worth asking for local advice on where to eat or enjoy local specialities. If you are lucky enough to be invited into a Hungarian home, be prepared for such treats as home-made paprika sausage or cold fat bacon laced with raw onion, in addition to other gastronomic delights.

*Éttrem* and *vendéglö* are the native words for restaurant. In Hungary the word 'restaurant' is only used of an establishment designed to attract foreigners, though this is changing. A *bisztro* has a limited range of dishes, while a *csárda*, originally the term for a modest inn, is now more likely to be a roadside place of some pretensions.

Mealtimes come round a little earlier than elsewhere in Europe because of the early start to the working day. This should present few problems to the visitor, though it may be difficult to get a meal late in the evening. Breakfasts are as substantial as you want them, usually a choice of eggs, cheese and sliced sausage or salami. Hungarians take their main meal at lunchtime and tend to eat cold snacks in the evening.

**Drinking**

Everyone has heard of Tokay and Bull's Blood and these wines are justifiably famous. But you are never far from a vineyard in Hungary and the country produces wine in quantity and of a quality to match its food. White wines prevail, though excellent, rather heavy reds come from the south of the country (Villány, Szekszárd) and lighter ones from around Sopron. Whites can be rather undistinguished, but there are many fine ones too, like the strong, very slightly sweet Badacsonyi, from the country's most spectacular vineyard among the old volcanoes on the north shore of Lake Balaton. The south-facing hills rising from the lake shore are among Europe's most interesting wine-producing areas, well worth exploring if only to see the delightful little wine-cellars dotted around the countryside, some of them built in 'peasant baroque' style. With good luck you might be invited to one of these to taste the wines made by the grower for himself and his friends. But there are plenty of more public ways of enjoying the variety of Hungarian wines; your hotel on Balaton may organise a tasting, or you may be able to sample the contents of the wine-cellar of the restaurant where you are eating.

The vines clothing the lower slopes of the mountains running northeast from Budapest produce mainly white wines, with the exception of the fruity and aromatic Bull's Blood from the area around Eger.

**Tokaj Treasure**

The little town of Tokaj produces one of the world's great wines. It is made from overripe grapes, crushed in seven-gallon tubs (*puttonyok*), and yielding an intensely sweet liquid which is added to barrels of more conventionally produced wine. The result can be a wine of 'silky texture and haunting fragrance' of increasing degrees of sweetness measured by the number of *puttonyok* per barrel (one to five). Tokay 'essence' is the tiny quantity of juice which has leaked naturally from the grapes while awaiting pressing. It ferments slowly and is supposedly endowed with miraculous powers. Traditionally reserved for the monarch on his deathbed, it is unlikely to be offered to the casual visitor!

Wine may be Hungary's national beverage, but spirits of highly individual character are made here too, most of them best treated with caution by the uninitiated. The best are fruit based, known generically as *palinka*; the plum yields *szilvapálinka* (like Czech or Yugoslav *slivovice*), the cherry *cseresznyepalinka*, the apricot *barackpálinka*. *Pálinka* from the Great Plain town of Kecskemét has a sound reputation, but the finest spirits come from private stills.

Should *pálinka* pall, beer (*sör*), or rather lager is universally available. Dark beers are also made by the country's surprisingly small number of breweries (five).

There is a good range of fruit juices, though fruit cordials tend to have a distinctly chemical flavour. Coffee is freely drunk and is good, usually in the form of espresso. As befits a country awash with spas, mineral water is available in great variety and can be a great help in coping with the spicy food.

A unique beverage to be tried is *Zwack Unicum*, designed ostensibly to aid the digestion (along the lines of German Underberg).

***Recommended beverages of Hungary***

## SHOPPING

The shopping scene has changed dramatically in recent years. In the old days, the range of consumer goods was relatively restricted, but those that were available (books, records, foodstuffs, ironmongery) represented fantastic value to the Western visitor. Nowadays anything can be bought in Hungary, especially in Budapest, but at a price which is often identical to what you would pay at home. Many bargains can still be found, however, some in the stores lining Budapest's glamorous main shopping artery, Váci utca, others in specialist shops.

Hungarian wines and spirits have a character all of their own (see **Food and Drink**). Groceries and delicatessens usually have a fair selection, or in Budapest you could try the specialised **Wine Store** at Házgyári utca 1 or even the shop which is part of the wine cellar in the **Hilton Hotel**. Delicacies like goose liver pâté (or goose liver itself), salami (particularly from Szeged and Gyula) and of course paprika could well feature on your list of less durable souvenirs.

Traditional products like carvings, pottery, embroidered blouses and tablecloths can be bought. The latter will be offered to you on the street by itinerant traders, some of them ethnic Hungarians from Transylvania, and there are specialist shops too like the **Folklore Centre** at Váci utca 14. More refined are the ceramics from the Zsolnay (Pécs) and Herend factories, though they may well cost the same as at home.

Hungarians are a bookish lot, and bookshops and stalls are to be found everywhere. Many foreign-language titles are published and are excellent value. The best places to find them in Budapest are at the bookstores at Váci utca 32 and Rákóczi utca 14. Antiquarian bookstores abound, many of them with foreign books. The **Owl** in Váci utca is one such.

The musically-minded will find themselves well catered for, with good quality, low-priced discs, cassettes and sheet music. Hungarian composers and performers feature prominently of course, and this is where to buy your definitive recordings of masters like Liszt, Bartók and Kodály. Make sure you listen as well to some of the amazing variety of folk music available.

Antique shops are no longer the haggler's paradise they may once have been, but are well stocked with items unlikely to be found at home. Budapest has a concentration of them in Néphadsereg utca north of the Parliament Building. A visit to an open-air market is likely to be rewarding, even if you do not buy. The lively flea market at Nagykörösi utca 156, way out in the southeastern suburbs of Budapest (bus 154) is open every day except Sundays, while its equivalent in Pécs (where you can buy a pig as well as a picture) takes place only on the first Sunday of each month.

Not just groceries and supermarkets but most shops expect you to pick up a wire basket on entry and carry it with you as you select your purchases.
Duty-free goods are available in hard-currency shops (Intertourist – in some of the main hotels – Utastourist and Konsumtourist).
Credit cards are accepted in an ever-growing number of places, but still less than in Western Europe or the US.
For sophisticated shopping try Budapest's department stores: one at Schönherz Z utca 6–10 in Buda, the biggest in the land, the other at Marx tér 1–2 in Pest.

## ACCOMMODATION

The range of places to stay in Hungary varies enormously, from 5-star hotels offering superb standards at somewhat more affordable prices than their Western equivalents, to extremely cheap tourist hostels with beds crammed against the walls and less than reliable plumbing.
More tourists visit Hungary than there are Hungarians. Demand is intense in the summer, and while local travel offices will do their best to help, it may be advisable to book ahead in the peak season.
Like so much else in the country, the tourist industry is in a state of flux. Parts of the nationalised sector, which include a number of the major hotels, face an uncertain future. The private sector is very active, but has yet to provide sufficient accommodation in the middle range, particularly in the capital. Pensions (*Panzió*) are often a good alternative to a hotel. Bed and breakfast in private homes (usually indicated by the German sign *'Zimmer frei'*) is widely available in holiday areas, and may be the best bargain in Budapest (though not always with breakfast!).
Do not be surprised to be charged more than the locals, though costs will still be lower than equivalent places in Western countries. Prices vary considerably, being highest in the capital and in the more attractive resorts around Lake Balaton, dropping off steeply elsewhere. For a longer stay it might be a good idea to rent an apartment or cottage.
Camping is well developed, and offers a good way of meeting locals and holidaymakers from other Eastern European countries. In summer, students and other young people can normally stay at very reasonable rates in the halls of residence attached to colleges and universities.
The accommodation information given in the guide can be supplemented by referring to the annual publications (*Hotel* and *Camping*) prepared by the Ministry of Tourism, which list and categorise hotels and campsites. Hungary abounds in tourist and travel agencies (some 1,000 in total, both state and private), most of which will help you find a place to stay. Of these, IBUSZ is the oldest, with offices in most towns (see **Directory – Tourist Offices**).

*Energetic folk dancers of Budapest*

## CULTURE, ENTERTAINMENT AND NIGHTLIFE

The intricacies of Hungarian will rule out theatre visits for most visitors from abroad, but there is much else on offer which transcends the language barrier. Hungary is a musical nation, and there is no dearth of concerts in cities and resorts, often in the pleasing setting of an outdoor auditorium or venerable church. Many, but by no means all such events are put on in the framework of an annual festival - see **Special Events**.

Music is not only performed for concert-goers; few restaurants of any pretension fail to have their resident gypsy band, with its *primas* (leader) wandering among the tables. Hungary's folk tradition is an extraordinarily rich one, a great inspiration to both Bartók and Kodály, and folk music is frequently heard, best of all in a *táncház*, one of the 'dance houses', which exist in most towns and which were the focus of the intense revival of folk which took place in the 1970s. Cimbalom, bagpipe, hurdy-gurdy and Jew's harp are some of the instruments accompanying the often wild dancing which takes place. Particularly in Budapest, you may find cinemas showing films in the original version with Hungarian subtitles.

Pop music is popular, and most towns have something to offer at the weekend in terms of live performances or at least a discotheque. The Balaton resorts, especially Siófok, have a fair range of entertainment of this kind, together with the occasional night club. Casinos are few and far between, at least outside Budapest.

See also **Entertainment** under Budapest, page 36.

## WEATHER AND WHEN TO GO

Hungary has a basically continental climate, but its long cold winters and long hot summers are tempered by Atlantic and Mediterranean influences. Conditions can change quite rapidly, and it is wise to be prepared for 'unseasonal' weather.

The sunshine record is good, up to an average of ten hours a day in the Balaton area in July, and temperatures tend to be slightly higher than in the surrounding countries. The summer season runs from May to September, so you do not have to go to Balaton in July and August when everybody else does!

Winters are foggy rather than snowy. Without high mountains, snow cannot be relied on, though skiing takes place in the Matra uplands. Summer heat is sometimes oppressive, particularly in cities with excessive air pollution. In particular, the local climate of Budapest, with its huge number of motor vehicles, can be very unpleasant.

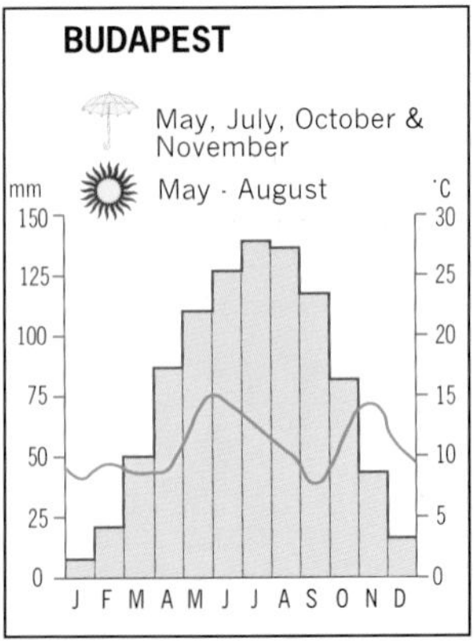

Tourism is possible all year round in Hungary, though provincial places may not be at their best in the winter months when many museums are closed. The best time to visit the country is on either side of the crowded main season, in the freshness of spring and in the autumn; remember that the grape harvest may not be completed until November in areas like Tokaj!

Theatres and the opera usually shut down for the summer.

## HOW TO BE A LOCAL

Hungarians have a long tradition of hospitality and the probability is that you will be made to feel welcome by the people you meet, sometimes embarrassingly so. Hosts may go to great lengths to ensure the well-being of their guests, not always consulting them in the process. 'Programmes' (an important word in Hungary) are likely to be arranged to show you the very best of what is available, not necessarily what you want to see. So it is as well to make your intentions clear at the start of any encounter.

The former regime did not encourage easy contacts with foreigners. Combined with the oppressive nature of life generally, this made many people cautious in their dealings with strangers. Do not be surprised therefore if some of the people you meet in a casual way are less than forthcoming, initially at least. A stony face may well conceal a warm heart!

Manners tend to be a formality which has been diluted in other countries, with much use of greetings (good morning, good afternoon, goodbye etc) even in the most casual situations (shops, restaurants).
Introductions are made in a formal way, with the use of titles like doctor and professor and with a handshake. If invited to someone's home, you should bring flowers or a small gift. You may well find yourself the recipient of gifts. Take care not to admire any of your hosts' possessions too much; they may feel impelled to offer them to you!
Hungarians take pleasure in eating and drinking and are eager for their guests to do the same. Toasts are common and glasses frequently refilled. It is advisable to monitor your consumption and only drink as much as you want to, when you want to. Good mineral water is always available if you are uncertain about the effects of apricot brandy!
The tradition which grew up under Communism of people having another job as well as their official one has continued and even intensified due to economic pressure. Earning a living absorbs a lot of time and energy and you should be careful about making demands on people which might disrupt their routine or eat into their small amount of free time.
Hungarian women do not have an easy life, shouldering the burden of work in exactly the same way as men and being expected to run their homes in a more or less traditional way as well.

*Colourful souvenirs on display*

*Fun at the fountain*

Hungarians look much like other Central Europeans, though there are some striking lookers whose facial features recall those of their ancestors from the steppes. A modified form of peasant garb is still worn by older people in parts of the countryside (aprons and headscarves for women, tough leather riding boots for men). Suits and ties are worn for business, but are not essential for theatre or opera going. Cigarette smoking is still accepted without question. The generosity and kindness extended to visitors is not always paralleled by tolerance of others nearer home. Suppression of any meaningful form of public debate under the old regime has left intact (or even intensified) attitudes which it is no longer respectable to admit to elsewhere. Nationalistic feelings are intense (not without reason), with Hungary and Hungarians cast in the role of perennial victim. The often unhappy history of the country is still felt deeply and frequently talked about, as is the exposed position of the substantial Hungarian minorities in neighbouring countries.

## CHILDREN

In a country with one of the lowest birthrates in the world (the population is actually declining), children enjoy a high status. For foreign children on holiday, Hungary offers a number of special attractions in addition to unusual features like caves and the usual activities to be found in, for example, the resorts around Lake Balaton. Displays of Hungarian horsemanship are likely to appeal to most young people; they can be experienced not only in the obvious places on the Great Plain like Hortobágy and Bugac-puszta, but elsewhere too. Local tourist offices will provide information about such activities and about other 'programmes' with a special appeal for children. Folklore performances have a lot of potential for entertaining at least some children, especially if there is a chance of taking part. Teenagers might enjoy a horseback trek across the *puszta* at Hortobágy, which lasts several days and involves sleeping under the stars. The more mechanically minded will respond to the narrow-gauge forest and agricultural railways still in operation in the Mátra and Bükk uplands as well as elsewhere in the country. One railway line, the Pioneer Railway through the Buda Hills, is actually staffed by children, who wear their miniature uniforms with pride (the engine driver, alas, is a grown-up). Busy Budapest, in some ways not an ideal environment for small children, nevertheless has a number of features which should appeal, some of them conveniently grouped in the City Park. Here is the **zoo**, with its amazing array of buildings and animals, the **Grand Circus**, and the somewhat shambolic **Amusement Park** (Vidámpark) with roller coaster and giant wheel. Budapest's two branches of the **National Puppet Theatre** (Állami Bábszínház, Andrássy ut 69 and Jókai tér 10) have performances for adults as well as for children.

## TIGHT BUDGET

To travel cheaply in Hungary you need to uncouple yourself from the international tourist circuit. Hungary can be a very economical holiday destination if you wish, even though prices are rising fast.

- Stay in private rooms or hostels, or camp.
- Buy picnic ingredients from shops and markets or eat in buffets or cafeterias.
- If you are staying in a hotel, you may well find that the big breakfast served will take you through most of the day.
- Check restaurant prices before entering – the same quality of food can vary considerably in price, depending on ambience and service and the target clientele.
- Nightlife in Budapest has recently been distinguished by greed on the part of the providers of services.
- If you have plenty of time, travel by public transport. A car may be the most convenient way of getting around, but petrol and hire cost the same as in Western Europe. In Budapest, trams, buses, trolleybuses and the Metro are very cheap. Taxis can overcharge, especially on the journey from the airport.
- Organised sightseeing tours which often include meals should be avoided. Trains and buses are very cheap and will take you to most parts of the country.
- The same kind of rules apply to entertainment and cultural life. 'Programmes' intended for foreigners will be relatively (not necessarily prohibitively) expensive, but concerts, the opera, museums and galleries still offer amazing value.
- Glossy gift shops may not be the best places to get your souvenirs. Go instead to the grocers or supermarket, the book or record store.

## SPECIAL EVENTS

An annual booklet *Programmes in Hungary*, giving details of events all over the country, is published each November by the Hungarian Tourist Board. The following is a selection from the very large number of such activities.

**January**
**Farshang** (Fasching), the New Year ball season (continues into February).

**February**
**Mohács:** Buso carnival, south Slav festival driving out winter and welcoming spring.
**Budapest:** festival of new Hungarian films ('Filmszemle').

*Entertainment in Vaci ut*

**March**
**Budapest Spring Festival**, a major international event, held not only in the capital but in a number of provincial centres as well. Concerts, opera performances, dance, folklore, theatre, master classes and exhibitions.

**Easter**
**Countrywide:** (notably at Hollókö) folk customs, painted eggs, splashing of girls and young women by bands of revellers.

**May**
**Budapest:** Book Week, bookstalls and booksigning by authors.

**June**
**Buják:** Palotian and Slovak folklore festival.

**Pécs:** start of Summer Festival, with open-air concert and theatre performances, cabaret, folklore of national minorities (German, Croat etc).
**Sopron:** Early Music Days (classical concerts).
**Budapest:** start of open-air performances on Margaret Island.
**Gyula Castle**: theatre evenings until mid-August.

### July

**Hortobágy:** International Equestrian Days.
**Kiskunság:** Pastoral and Equestrian Days.
**Szeged:** open-air Festival, opera, theatre, folklore (continues into August).
**Martonvásár** (southwest of Budapest): Beethoven concerts in grounds of Brunsvick Castle.
**Szentendre:** weekend fairs (continue into August).

### August

**Hortobágy:** Bridge Fair (19–20 August).
**Debrecen:** Floral Carnival (last week of August).
**Hungaroring** (northeast of Budapest): Hungarian Grand Prix.
**Countrywide:** St Stephen's Day (20 August) celebrations, fairs, processions, folklore, fireworks (notably in Budapest).

### September

**Budapest:** Budapest Arts Weeks, concerts, theatre, dance, art exhibitions (continues into October).
**Badacsony:** Vintage Festival (21–2 September).
**Szombathely:** Savaria Autumn Festival (mid-September to early October).

## SPORT

Most sports are practised in Hungary, save those dependent on a coastline or high mountains. The country is especially attractive for riders and hunters, but golfing is in its infancy.

Spectator sports not unnaturally include football, the most spectacular setting for which is the huge postwar Népstadion in Budapest. Next to this national stadium is the Sportcsarnok, a multi-purpose hall with a capacity of 10,000 people, used for many sporting events (including ice-hockey) as well as other gatherings like concerts and conferences.

Completed in 1986, the Hungaroring motor-racing circuit just to the northeast of the capital attracts big crowds, especially for the Hungarian Grand Prix in August.

Both flat-racing and trotting take place in Budapest, the former at Kincsem park, the latter at the Ügetöpálya. The crowd may excite your attention as much as the horses!

Horsemanship of a more participatory kind can be practised all over the country: riding schools, studs and stables abound. The fenceless *puszta* has obvious attractions, but trekking holidays are organised in many areas like the hill country to the north of Lake Balaton or the Danube Bend. Further details are in the Hungarian Tourist Board's brochure *Riding*.

Hungary's varied landscapes are rich in game. With a permit you can pursue boar and deer as well as partridge and pheasant, waterfowl, hare and rabbit. Hunting is well organised, attracting large numbers of visitors from abroad, and packages are available. Useful information is given in the brochure *Hunting* published by the Hungarian Tourist Board.

Anglers, armed with a permit, can hook pike, perch and carp and 40+ other species from lakes (Balaton, Velence, Rakaca) and rivers (arms of the Danube in the northwest and downstream from Budapest, the Tisza near Tiszalök).

The lack of a seaside means that the country's water resources are exploited to the full, above all on Balaton, with its myriad sailing boats, but also on the other lakes and rivers. Canoeing holidays are popular. Details of how to hire boats and equipment are given in the Tourist Board's *Water Tours in Hungary*. Most towns and many hotels have swimming pools.

In winter, ice-skating is practised in many places. The hundreds of brightly-clad skaters swirling around the large rink at the Heroes' Square entrance to the City Park in Budapest make a splendid spectacle. The shallow waters of Lakes Balaton and Velence freeze over for long periods, though the movement of the ice means that skating is not always possible. Hungarian skiers head north to the guaranteed snow of the Tatra and Fatra Mountains in neighbouring Slovakia, but nearer home there are runs in the Mátra uplands and even just outside Budapest (at Normafa).

***The splendid Secessionist swimming pool at Gellért Hotel offers the perfect setting for exercise***

# Directory

*This section (with the biscuit-coloured band) contains day-to-day information, including travel, health and documentation.*

**Contents**



## Arriving

### Entry Formalities

Nationals of most European countries, Canada and the US no longer require a visa to enter Hungary, merely a valid passport (identity card in the case of Germany). Visitors needing a visa may obtain it, normally within 24 hours, at Hungarian embassies or consulates in their own country. Alternatively, a visa may be requested at highway border crossings, Budapest (Ferihegy) Airport and the International Landing Stage (NB not at rail crossings), but the fee is much higher. Visas are issued for a maximum stay of 90 days.

Registration with the local police is now only necessary for visitors staying in private accommodation for a period of more than 30 days.

### By Air

About 12 miles (20km) from Budapest city centre, Ferihegy Airport is linked to most major cities in Europe by the main international airlines as well as by the Hungarian national airline, MALEV. MALEV passengers use Terminal 2 (completed in 1985), all others Terminal 1. The airport has the usual services (car hire, duty free, post office etc).
A shuttle bus links both terminals at half-hourly intervals

(06.00–22.00hrs) with the Erzsébet tér bus station in Pest. Travel time is 30 mins (Terminal 1), 40 mins (Terminal 2). An alternative is bus no 93 which connects with the Metro terminus at Köbánya Kispest. Taxis are readily available (but beware of overcharging). Internal flights in Hungary were discontinued several years ago, but attempts to reopen at least some of them are in the offing. MALEV has offices in both terminals and in Budapest city centre (Roosevelt tér 2, tel: 117 2911). Reservations can be made by phone (tel: 118 4333) Monday to Friday 08.00–17.00hrs, Saturday 07.30–14.00hrs.

### By Rail

Budapest occupies a central position in the European rail network and trains run direct to many foreign cities. Inter-Rail cards are valid for Hungary and represent excellent value. MÁV (Hungarian State Railways) information is available in Budapest, tel: 122 4052. You will normally need to supplement your ordinary ticket with a seat reservation bought in advance. Travellers to and from Western Europe will use – perhaps confusingly – the East (Keleti) station in Budapest.

### By Bus

Coach services link Budapest's central bus station in Erzsébet tér and Balaton resorts with a large number of destinations in neighbouring countries and in Germany (Vienna twice daily, Munich twice weekly). Information, tel: 117 2562.

### By Boat

MAHART (Hungarian Shipping Co) operates a daily hydrofoil linking Budapest and Vienna between April and September. The international landing stage is on the Danube Promenade (Belgrád rakpart) in Pest, between Elisabeth Bridge and Freedom Bridge. Information, tel: 118 1758.

*Nyugati station in Budapest*

**Camping**
Hungary is well provided with camping facilities. Sites exist in all parts of the country, including Budapest, with a particular concentration around Lake Balaton. Sites are graded into three categories according to facilities; many sites offer other types of accommodation as well, like 'bungalows' (ie chalets). Prices are less in the low season and reductions may be made for holders of the FICC-AIT-IA camping carnet or student card. A map and list giving details of all sites is published annually.

**Crime**
Crime was once notable by its absence. Though the situation has changed for the worse, Hungary is still a safer place to be in than most Western countries. Visitors need take no more than the usual measures to ensure their own safety and that of their property.
Bear in mind that sophisticated items like cameras or video equipment (to say nothing of a wallet stuffed with hard currency) may be worth the equivalent of several months local salary. Remove tempting objects from your car and lock it on leaving. Watch for pickpockets in markets, crowded shopping areas and main railway stations.
Drinking and driving continues to attract harsh penalties.

**Customs Regulations**
Procedures have been much simplified in recent years and are unlikely to cause any bother to *bona fide* travellers. Delays are unlikely to be long except at road crossings with Austria at peak times. You may bring into Hungary all the personal belongings you need for your stay, but they must be taken with you when you leave the country. Duty free allowances include: 250 cigarettes or 50 cigars or 250 grammes of tobacco; 2 litres of wine; 1 litre of spirits; other goods worth more than 5,000 forints (500 forints in the case of a second or subsequent entry) must be declared and are liable to duty (25 per cent VAT must be paid on goods subject to customs duty).

**Disabled Travellers**
Hungary has lagged behind Western European countries in adapting the environment to respond to the needs of the disabled. Public buildings and public transport rarely have special facilities, and though this may be compensated for by personal helpfulness, this should obviously not be relied on. Exceptions to the general rule can be found in spa resorts.

**Driving**
Only those documents required in the visitor's own country are needed (driving licence, vehicle registration, insurance certificate). A first-aid kit and warning triangle should be carried and a nationality sticker or plate attached.
The road network in Hungary is reasonably well developed and maintained. Main roads radiate from Budapest and many cross-country journeys are quicker if made via the capital. Modern highways reach all parts of the

country. Every settlement with a population of more than 200 people is accessible by a surfaced road. Motorway mileage is limited: the Budapest–Vienna link should be completed by 1995, but a long section of this major highway is still an ordinary (and frequently overcrowded) two-lane road, as is part of the busy Budapest–Miskolc link. Road signs correspond to international norms. Direction signs are generally, but not always, reliable, sometimes indicating the first village along the way rather than a major destination. At night and at other times when there is little traffic, the normal sequence of traffic lights may be replaced by a flashing amber light; you must then observe whatever priority is indicated by the normal traffic signs (yellow diamond = priority, inverted red/white triangle = give way).

***Renting a car in Hungary should pose no problems since several international firms have branches there***

The mix of road users can be a volatile one, ranging from horse-drawn vehicles to local boys made good, who obviously feel that a new BMW grants immunity from speed restrictions. Budapest drivers are often described as 'nervous'. Slow-moving lorries can cause problems, especially in winter, when accumulated filth is thrown up from the road surface.

Traffic is heavy in Budapest and hold-ups frequent. Parking is difficult (multi-storey car-parks in Martinelli tér and Aranykéz utca) and cars without a permit (hotel residents qualify for one) are banned from Castle Hill and parts of the inner city. Use of the public transport system is highly advisable. Trams share the roadway and unless traffic lights give a clear indication to the contrary, should be given priority.

Round-the-clock information on road and traffic conditions is available from Utinform Highway Information Centre, Budapest, Dob utca 75 (tel: 122 7052/7643).

**Traffic Regulations**
The normal rule of driving on the right and overtaking on the left applies in Hungary, but is frequently ignored on dual carriageway roads in towns, where drivers hugging the outside lane are often overtaken on the inside.
The speed limits for cars are lower than in most European countries, but are appropriate for Hungarian conditions and are meant to be observed. They are as follows:

- on motorways, 120kph
- on other limited-access highways, 100kph
- on other roads, 80kph
- in built-up areas, 60kph (indicated by the sign giving the place-name).

Safety-belts must be worn. Children under 12 are not allowed to travel in the front seat of a car. Motorcyclists must wear helmets and use dipped headlights in the daytime.
There is an absolute prohibition on drinking – even the smallest amount – and driving. A driver with a blood alcohol level of more than 0.008 is considered to have committed a criminal offence.

**Accidents and Assistance**
The police must be called if any accident involves an injury (see **Emergency Telephone Numbers**, page 114). It is also advisable to contact them if there is disagreement about responsibility for an accident. Accidents involving insurance claims should be reported within 48 hours to the International Vehicle Insurance Office in Budapest, Gvadányi ut 69 (tel: 183 5350), or to the local vehicle insurance office.
In case of breakdown, the 'yellow angels' of the Magyar Autoklub (head office in Budapest, Rómer Flóris utca 4/a, tel: 115 1220 or 252 8000 for emergency service) will render assistance, either free or at reduced rates for members of affiliated national automobile organisations. The M7 Budapest –Balaton motorway has emergency aid telephones at 1.25-mile (2km) intervals.

**Fuel**
The provision of petrol stations is adequate, if not lavish. You may have to wait for service for a few minutes at busy times. Fuel is available at octane ratings of 86, 92 (super) and 98 (extra). Lead-free, 95 octane, (often indicated by its German name 'bleifrei') is distributed from a growing number of outlets.

**Car Rental**
The well-known international car-hire firms have arrangements with local agencies. Avis, for example, is linked with IBUSZ, the old established Hungarian travel company (founded 1902), whose network of 90 offices covers the whole of the country. Normal rental conditions apply: the driver must be over 21, have held a licence for more than a year, etc. Payment must be made in hard currency, though you can use a credit card. Most hire cars will now be familiar Western models. It is worthwhile checking in advance whether a vehicle is available.

**Electricity**
The voltage of the electricity supply in Hungary is 220 volts AC. Appliances fitted with British or US plugs will require an adapter if they are to be used in local sockets, which are of the standard continental European type.

**Embassies**
**UK:** Budapest V, Harmincad utca 6, tel: 118 2888.
**US:** Budapest V, Szabadság tér 12, tel: 112 6450.
**Australia:** Budapest VI, Délibáb utca 30, tel: 153 4233.
**Canada:** Budapest XII, Budakeszi út 32, tel: 176 7711.

**Emergency Telephone Numbers**
**Police (Rendörség)**: 07
**Fire:** 05
**Ambulance:** 04

**Entertainment Information**
The Hungarian Tourist Board's monthly *Programme in Ungarn/in Hungary* covers entertainment and events in Budapest and the provinces. The English language *Budapest Week* boasts a complete 'Entertainment Guide' which includes listings of foreign - language films in Budapest cinemas. See also **Special Events**, page 106, and **Entertainment** in the Budapest section of the guide.

**Health**
The water supply is well managed in Hungary and water is generally quite safe to drink, even though you should sample the wide range of bottled mineral waters available. Hygienic conditions in toilets vary from the impeccable to the abysmal, with a good average standard in most places. Fruit and vegetables are sold in a defiantly unwashed condition (perhaps as proof of their recent harvesting) and need to be washed before eating.

**Medical Care**
First aid and transport to hospital is provided free. Further treatment may be charged, though citizens are entitled to free emergency care. It is sensible to take out travel insurance which includes health cover. You will normally be able to find an English-speaking doctor easily.

**Spas**
Hungary is uniquely endowed with over one thousand medicinal hot springs and no fewer than 22 towns and 62 smaller places officially designated as spas. In each of them, the special curative properties of the local waters are put to work as part of complex therapy programmes designed to treat a great variety of medical conditions.
Budapest, known as the 'city of spas', has more than 30 thermal springs, harnessed in such contrasting settings as the domed Turkish Király Baths, the Art Nouveau underworld of the extraordinary Gellért Hotel, or the flamboyant Victorian architecture of the Széchenyi Spa in the City Park. The luxuriously appointed spas of western Hungary, foremost among them the great thermal lake at Hévíz, attract visitors from Austria and Germany, but few places in the country are far from healing waters.

A 'cure' at a Hungarian spa is likely to be not only a healing but also an entertaining experience, with plenty of recreational facilities at hand and hotels and local travel agencies eager to arrange excursion 'programmes' for you. Further details about spas and what they offer are available in *Spas in Hungary*, published by the Hungarian Tourist Board.

### Holidays – Public and Religious

1 January: New Year's Day; 15 March: Day of the Nation – commemorates the outbreak of the 1848 Revolution; Easter Monday; 1 May: Labour Day; 20 August: St Stephen's Day (see **Special Events**, page 106); 23 October: anniversary of the 1956 uprising and, since 1989, the change in the country's official designation, from 'People's Republic' to 'Republic'; 25–26 December.

### Lost Property

A variety of offices in Budapest deal with lost property, depending on where it was lost.
**City transport:** BKV, Akácfa u 18, tel: 122 6613.
**Railway**: East (Keleti) Station, left luggage office, tel: 122 5615; South (Déli) Station, track 12, tel: 175 9485; West (Nyugati) Station, tel: 149 0115.
**Taxi:** Fötaxi, Akácfa u 20, tel: 134 4704; Volántaxi, Jerney u 56, tel: 163 3228; other firms, tel: 117 4961.
**Plane:** Ferihegy 1, tel: 147 2784; Ferihegy 2, tel: 157 8108.
The **Central Lost and Found Office** is at Erzsébet tér 5, tel: 117 4961.

### Media

#### Press

The long-established *English Daily News* with its coverage of international and local news and events, despite its name, only appears weekly. *Budapest Week* is a weekly review of Hungarian affairs, primarily for English-speaking residents but with much to interest the visitor, including entertainment listings. *The Hungarian Observer*, in *Newsweek/Spiegel* format, has good business and political coverage and a pull-out section with cultural and entertainment listings. The *New Hungarian Quarterly* is heavy by comparison, a magazine of international stature, with in-depth articles by authorities on their subjects. Foreign-language papers and periodicals are available late on the day of publication if you are lucky, at hotels and some newsagents (commonly found in stations).

*Souvenirs are abundant*

### Radio and TV

**Radio Danubius** broadcasts news in English at 13.30 and 19.30hrs, **Petőfi Radio** at noon. Hungarian TV has taken to transmitting the BBC News with Hungarian subtitles at 23.00 hrs on Channel One, on Monday, Tuesday, Thursday and Friday. Most large hotels have cable TV with Sky and Superchannel.

## Money Matters

The unit of currency is the forint, subdivided into 100 worthless fillers. Until you get used to them, prices have a somewhat astronomical appearance.
Coins are in denominations of 10, 20 and 50 fillers (you will not find much to buy with these) and 1, 2, 5, 10 and 20 forints. Most purchases involve the use of banknotes, which come in denominations of 10, 20, 50, 100, 500, 1,000 and, introduced recently with quite a stir, 5,000 forints.
The forint is not yet freely convertible, and you are not permitted to bring in or take out more than trivial amounts (500 forints). It is rare to have difficulty in changing convertible currencies: banks, travel offices, hotels are happy to help, as are the touts who will approach you on the street. Avoid their offers; black market exchanges are illegal, and scams are commonplace – you may well end up with a 'sandwich' of toilet paper as the filling, inside real notes (the bread). Do not be extravagant in changing: you are only allowed to reconvert up to half of what you have exchanged, and that only with a proper receipt. Given the ease of changing, it is probably best to renew your supplies of Hungarian cash every few days, as and when you need it rather than in one big lump at the start of your stay.
Credit cards are in ever-increasing use, particularly in hotels and other places frequented by more affluent foreigners, but are by no means acceptable everywhere; check before choosing.
Eurocheques may be used up to a limit of 15,000 forints.

## Opening Times

### Shops

Shopping hours are fairly consistent around the country. While non-food shops open 10.00–18.00hrs, food shops open 07.00–19.00hrs. There may be late shopping on Thursdays. Saturday afternoon is early closing and few shops (apart from some department stores) remain open after 14.00hrs. Some food shops open on Sunday mornings and there is a growing number of round-the-clock groceries in the capital. Shops in smaller places often close for a lunch break in the middle of the day. The annoying habit of closing unannounced for an 'inventory' seems to be less frequent than it once was.
Local markets start and end early, usually 06.00–13.00hrs.

### Museums

Open every day except Mondays and some holidays, mostly 10.00–18.00hrs. Museums in smaller or remote places may keep shorter hours, and many such establishments are closed in winter (including virtually all the *skansens* or open-air museums).

### Personal Safety

There are no special problems with personal security in Hungary. In a few remote areas an obvious foreigner may attract some curiosity, but this is unlikely to be anything other than innocent. See also **Crime**.

### Pharmacies

Pharmacies in Hungary have a venerable pedigree, and almost every town has its historic *Gyógyszertár*, full of archaic medicine bottles and other pharmaceutical impedimenta. For your current minor ailments, the modern pharmacy is likely to have a remedy, at a considerably lower cost than at home. A jug of water and glass are thoughtfully provided for you to take your medicine on the spot. One of the pharmacists will probably speak German if not English.

### Places of Worship

Roman Catholics form the majority of practising Christians in Hungary, but there is a substantial Protestant minority, and the Orthodox Church is represented too. The country's remaining Jews are concentrated in Budapest; many synagogues have been converted to some other use. Services are generally well attended. The usual decorum should be observed when visiting. Churches are often locked – a hand-written note on the door will usually indicate where the keeper of the key can be found.

The following Budapest churches have services in English:

**International Church of Budapest**, Buda Cultural Centre, Corvin tér 8, tel: 136 4518. 10.30hrs every Sunday.

**Scottish Mission Church**, Vörösmarty utca 51. Every Sunday at 11.00hrs.

**Jesuit Church of the Sacred Heart**, Mária utca 25, tel: 118 3479. Every Saturday at 17.00hrs.

### Police

The Hungarian police force (*Rendörség*) is organised nationally rather than locally. Uniforms are blue-grey, with white trim for traffic police. Officers, while helpful, are unlikely to speak English but may have a reasonable knowledge of German. Nowadays their distinctively marked patrol cars are more likely to be of German than Soviet origin. (See also **Emergency Telephone Numbers** and **Driving**.)

### Post Office

Most post offices are open 08.00–19.00hrs Monday to Friday and until 13.00hrs on Saturday. Two round-the-clock post offices operate in Budapest, one near the West (Nyugati) Station at Terez körút 105–7, the other near the East (Keleti) Station at Baross tér 11/c.

It may be less time-consuming buying your stamps at a tobacco kiosk than queuing at the post office.

*Rural post office*

A superior international service for telegrams, faxes and telexes is available at the Budapest Post Service Centre at Petőfi S utca 17–19, open: Monday to Friday 07.00–21.00hrs, Saturday 07.00–20.00hrs and Sunday morning 08.00–13.00hrs.

## Public Transport

### Rail

Any place in Hungary that can be remotely described as a town is accessible by the trains of MÁV (Hungarian State Railways) – though it may take time! The best services are the express trains linking Budapest with the major provincial centres; these depart from the splendid 19th-century West (Nyugati) or East (Keleti) Stations in Pest, or the completely rebuilt South (Déli) Station in Buda. They may have a 'comfort' carriage attached offering additional amenities for a small supplementary fare. Because the rail network focuses on Budapest, it may well be quicker to make a cross-country journey via the capital. Connections onward to smaller places are likely to be by trains made up of four-wheel diesel railcars, robust enough but hardly the last word in travel comfort. A pleasing anomaly in the state-dominated network is the old GySEV line between Győr, Sopron and Ebenfürth in Austria, an independent railway which somehow continued to operate across the Austrian border all through the Communist era.

Fares, though rising, are still very low, and you might consider travelling in the comfort of first class, even if you would not dream of it at home. The whole or part of an international journey will have to be paid for in hard currency. MÁV offer numerous concessionary fares, including 7- and 10-day Rail Cards giving unlimited travel over the whole network, a Balaton Card for the lines around the great lake, reductions for young and old and for people travelling in groups. You will normally need to make a seat reservation for longer-distance trains.

MÁV's timetable (which comes with a comprehensive map of the rail network) is considerately written in five languages. Other information is best obtained from their Passenger Service in Budapest, at Andrássy út 35, tel: 118 2430.

### Bus and Coach

Rail services are supplemented by long-distance coaches, which may well get you there faster, though possibly more expensively. The main terminal in Budapest is in Erzsébet tér. It is a good idea to check your journey and buy your ticket a good day in advance.

The main operator is nationalised Volán *('wheel')*, whose yellow buses are operated by county divisions of the company. Local services are supposed to reach every settlement in the country with a population of more than 200, though they may run infrequently or at inconvenient times. Urban bus lines are equally comprehensive.

### Taxis

There is over-provision of taxis in most places in Hungary. State and private firms compete and you should have no difficulty in finding a cab, either in ranks on the street, by hailing a vehicle with its roof sign illuminated, or by telephoning. Check that the taxi has a meter and that it is switched on. Overcharging has unfortunately become commonplace.

The biggest cab company in Budapest is Fötaxi, tel: 122 2222.

### Boats and Ferries

Where traffic volumes are low, and where distances between high flood embankments have made bridge construction uneconomic, river ferries operate, particularly in Eastern Hungary, but also on the Danube. Csepel Island, for example, can only be reached from the west by ferry, and an excursion to the Danube Bend can be made more interesting by using ferries to switch from one bank to the other. On Lake Balaton, the ferry across the straits between Tihany and Szántód is particularly busy. In remoter areas, ferries may be hand-hauled and require some skill in negotiating your vehicle aboard (mostly on the part of the ferryman!).

Regular boat services operate on both Danube and Balaton except in the winter months. The towns along the Danube Bend to Esztergom are a popular destination. There are evening pleasure cruises too. For information on boat services and trips from Budapest from Vigadó tér landing stage, tel: 129 8844 or 118 1223; in the Balaton resorts at all the landing stages, eg Balatonfüred, tel: 86/42 230 or Siófok, tel: 84/10 050.

### Transport in Budapest

Run by BKV (Budapest City Transport), the capital's public transport system is one of the most effective in the world, though not held in particularly high esteem by those residents who have to travel regularly in the rush hour. Its Metro, trams, buses, trolleybuses and suburban railways will get you to all parts of the metropolis cheaply and reliably throughout most of the day and there are night services as well. The network is set out in detail on the map issued by BKV, a very useful aid.

Tickets (flat fare) must be purchased before travel from

tobacconists, kiosks, Metro stations, bus terminals or dispensers, then validated by cancelling them in one of the machines aboard every vehicle or on entering the Metro; they are valid for an hour after starting your trip.

Most locals have a monthly pass, but day passes are also available (a two-week ticket needs a photo).

*A delightful way to see Budapest*

There are three Metro lines, colour-coded red, yellow and blue, linking all three main stations and intersecting at Deák tér in the centre of Pest. Some of the stations are deep underground, reached by spectacularly long escalators.

Trams offer a better view of the sights, particularly those which run along the Little Boulevard or on both banks of the Danube. Appreciating this, BKV operate vintage trams on the riverside lines during the summer.

Many buses are of the articulated type, their long, blue concertina bodies as much a part of the townscape as the bright yellow trams. Special minibuses link Castle Hill with the important transport interchange (trams, buses, metro) at Moszkva tér.

The suburban railway (HEV) serves a number of useful destinations beyond the city boundary, including Szentendre (from the Batthyány tér terminus) and Ráckeve on Csepel Island (from the Vágóhíd terminus).

Two other modes of Budapest transport are likely to appeal to the visitor. The old Sikló (funicular), wrecked in the 1944–5 siege, has recently been fully restored to its former glory, and will haul you smoothly from the end of the Chain Bridge up to Castle Hill, while the equally venerable cogwheel railway, starting from its lower terminus at Városmajor, climbs through exclusive villa suburbs to the fresh air of the Buda Heights at Széchenyi Hill.

Finally, both banks of the

Danube and Margaret Island are linked by regular boat services, on which tram and bus tickets can be used.

### Senior Citizens

Some concessions are available for visitors, such as reduced rail fares (for women over 55, men over 60). Taxis are a feasible alternative to public transport queues and crowding, luxury hotels still less expensive than at home. A spa holiday can be highly recommended to all citizens, however senior! – see **Health** (page 114).

### Student and Youth Travel

Rail travel concessions are made to young people under 26. Details from the **Express Agency** which specialises in youth and student travel (Express Utazási Iroda, Budapest V, Beloiannisz u 10, tel: 111 6418).
Express also arranges accommodation in hostels and, outside term-time (particularly during the July–August holiday), in college halls of residence. This is best booked well in advance. The Express office in the capital is at Budapest V, Semmelweiss u 4, tel: 117 6634 or 117 8600, and there is also an office in the East (Keleti) Station. Canteen meals are usually available in halls of residence.

### Telephones

Hungary has direct dialling for domestic and international calls, though more than one try is sometimes necessary before you get through. International calls can be made from the red telephones.
Local calls: wait for tone, insert coin (minimum 5 forints), dial.
Long-distance calls within Hungary: wait for dialling tone, insert coin(s), dial 06, wait for change of tone, dial area code, then subscriber's number.
International calls: wait for dialling tone, insert coin(s), dial 00, wait for change of tone, dial international code, area code and subscriber's number.
Calls are cheaper between 18.00 and 07.00hrs. It may be more restful to telephone from your hotel, though you will pay an enhanced daytime rate for all calls.
Budapest Directory Inquiries in foreign languages, tel: 117 2200 (weekdays).

### Time

Hungary uses Central European Time, one hour ahead of Greenwich Mean Time. Clocks change for daylight saving in the last weekend of April and the last weekend of September.

### Tipping

Rules for tipping are similar to those in other countries, 10 per cent or perhaps slightly more being the conventional amount to add to taxi fares, restaurant bills etc.

### Toilets

Public lavatories can be found in bus terminals, railway stations and at a few other places, but those in bars, cafés and hotels are likely to be more attractive. Gents is indicated by *férfi*, ladies by *nöi*. You should leave a coin in the saucer at the entrance (especially if paper has been provided!).

## Tourist Offices

### Abroad

**UK:** Danube Travel, 6 Conduit Street, London W1R 9TG, tel: 071 493 0263.
**US:** Ibusz (North American Division), One Parker Plaza Suite 1104, Fort Lee, NJ 07024, tel: (1 201) 592 8585; Ibusz (Midewst Office) 233 North Michigan Avenue, Suite 1308, Chicago, IL 60601, tel: (1 312) 819 3150
**Germany:** Ibusz, 102 Berlin 0, Karl Liebknecht Str 9-11, tel: (37 2) 212 35 59

### In Hungary

**Tourinform** in Budapest V, Sütö utca 2 (near Deák tér Metro), tel: 117 9800, open from 08.00–20.00hrs, has a multilingual staff eager to dispense their wealth of information on anything you are likely to need to know.

The country is extremely well supplied with tourist offices and travel agencies (more than 1,000 in all) in both Budapest and the provinces, though the information they supply may fall short of your requirements. Senior among them is IBUSZ, founded in 1902, with branches in every place of consequence, but there are several others organised on a national (such as Cooptourist, Volántourist) or county basis. Most towns and resorts have several such offices, competing with each other to provide you with information of all kinds as well as arranging accommodation and 'programmes'.
In Budapest, IBUSZ has a round-the-clock room-finding service at Petöfi tér 3 (behind the Intercontinental Hotel), tel: 118 5707.

*A timeless form of travel*

## LANGUAGE

Hungarian is a difficult language, little studied (let alone mastered) by foreigners. Native speakers do not expect to communicate with you in their own tongue. Most educated people are fluent in at least one other language, if not several; German is the main language of tourism, while English seems to be more popular among younger people. Under Communism, Russian was a compulsory school subject, but you will be hard put to find anyone admitting to speaking it. English will suffice if you stick to the main tourist circuit. The larger hotels and most tourist information centres will have an English-speaker available. Elsewhere, it might be a good idea to brush up any German you know and to learn at least a few basic words and phrases in Hungarian.
Apart from a few international words (*telefon*, *posta*), Hungarian offers you few clues to its meaning. This is because it is wholly unrelated to any other European language except Finnish and Estonian (and even they are very distant cousins). Hungarians are proud of its distinctiveness, its subtlety and its expressive power.
Whatever the difficulties of the language, it is always worthwhile learning a basic minimum. Not only do signs, directions and labels begin to make sense, but your efforts to communicate will give much pleasure to your hosts! Make sure you do not confuse surnames with first names; the latter always come second when written or spoken .

### Pronunciation

Unlike English, Hungarian pronunciation is regular and letters consistently stand for the same sounds. Nor are there any great variations between the way the language is spoken in different parts of the country; dialects are virtually unknown.

### Vowels

**a** without an accent, like o in hot
**á** long a as in car
**é** ay as in hay
**i** ee as in see
**ó** awe
(Ask a Hungarian to say Hollókö)
**ö** er
**ö** er (longer than ö)
**ú** oo as in food
**ü** like French u or German u
**u** longer than ü

### Consonants

**c** like ts in pets
**cs** like ch in chum
**gy** like j in jam, but quicker and lighter
**j** like y in yes
**ly** like y in yes
**ny** like ni in onion
**s** like sh
**sz** like s in so
**zs** like s in pleasure

### Useful Words

**állomás** station
**áruház** supermarket, department store
**bejárat** entrance
**belváros** town centre
**bolt** shop
**bor** wine
**Borozó** wine bar
**busz** bus
**csárda** inn
**csemege** delicatessen

**cukrászda** pastry shop
**domb** hill
**étterem** restaurant
**falu** village
**fel** up
**felvilágositás** information
**ferfi WC** men's toilets
**fö** main (**fö tér** main square)
**foglalt** reserved, occupied
**forró** hot
**fürdö** bath, spa
**gyógyszertár** pharmacy
**gyümölcs** fruit
**hegy** hill
**híd** bridge
**hideg** cold
**húzni** pull
**italbolt** local bar
**kapu** door, town gate
**kastély** manor house, chateau
**kemping** camp site
**kert** garden
**kijárat** exit
**kis** little
**komp** ferry
**könyvesbolt** bookshop
**körút** boulevard
**le** down
**megálló** public transport stop
**mozi** cinema
**nagy** big
**nöi** WC ladies' toilets
**nyitva** open
**pályaudvar** (often shortened to **pu**) railway station
**panzio** pension, guest-house
**patika** pharmacy
**pénztár** cash desk, booking office
**piac** market
**pihenöhely** service area (motorway)
**pince** cellar
**rendörség** police
**rom** ruin
**sör** beer
**sörözö** beer-hall, brasserie
**strand** beach
**szabad** vacant, free
**szálloda** hotel
**színház** theatre
**szoba** room
**szoba kiadó** 'bed and breakfast' (literally room to let)
**tánc** dance
**templom** church
**tér** square
**tilos** prohibited
**tilos a belépés** no entry
**tilos a dohányzás** no smoking
**tó** lake
**tolni** push
**torony** tower
**új** new
**út** avenue
**utca** (often shortened to u) road, street
**vám** customs
**vár** castle
**város** town
**vendéglö** restaurant
**veszély** danger
**véskijárat** emergency exit
**villamos** tram
**vigyázat** caution
**víz** water
**zárva** closed
**zöldség** vegetables
**zsinagóga** synagogue

**Basic Words and Phrases**

**yes** igen
**no** nem
**please** kérem
**thank you (very much)** köszönöm (szépen)
**do you speak English?** beszél angolul?
**do you speak German?** beszél németül?
**I do not understand** nem értem
**I am English (American)** angol/amerikai vagyok
**good morning** jó reggelt kivánok (kivánok = I wish you, is optional)
**good day** jó napot kivánok

**good evening** jó estét
**good night** jó éjszakát
**hello!** szia! *or* szervusz! (confusingly, can mean cheerio! as well)
**goodbye** viszontlátásra
**sorry** sajnálom
**where? (is)** hol? (van)
**how?** hogy?
**how much?** mennyi?
**when?** mikor?
**who?** ki?
**what?** mi?

**Numbers**

0 nulla
1 egy
2 kettö
3 három
4 négy
5 öt
6 hat
7 hét
8 nyolc
9 kilenc
10 tíz
11 tízenegy
12 tízenkettö
13 tízenhárom
14 tízennégy
15 tízenöt
16 tízenhat
17 tízenhét
18 tízennyolc
19 tízenkilenc
20 húsz
21 huszonegy
30 harminc
40 negyven
50 ötven
60 hatvan
70 hetven
80 nyolcvan
90 kilencven
100 száz
1,000 egyezer

**Days of the Week**

**Monday** Hétfö
**Tuesday** Kedd
**Wednesday** Szerda
**Thursday** Csütörtök
**Friday** Péntek
**Saturday** Szombat
**Sunday** Vasárnap

**Months of the Year**

Happily, these are recognisable: Január, Február, Március, Április, Május, Június, Július, Augusztus, Szeptember, Október, November, December.

*St Stephen is widely commemorated in Hungary*

**INDEX**
Page numbers in *italic* refer to illustrations

**Acknowldegements**
The Automobile Association would like to thank the following photographers and libraries for their assistance in the preparation of this book:

**Eric Meacher and Peter Wilson** took all the pictures not mentioned below;

**Mary Evans Picture Library** 10 Matthias Corvinus, 14 Magyars;

**Nature Photographers Ltd** 89 Ciconia Ciconia (M E Gore), 90 Tree Frog, 93 Great Spotted Woodpecker, 94 Spiked Speedwell (P R Sterry);

**World Pictures** *cover* Traditional costume